Talking with Angels of Love

Talking with Angels of Love

Open your Heart

AMANDA HART

First published in Great Britain in 2020 by Orion Spring
an imprint of The Orion Publishing Group Ltd
Carmelite House, 50 Victoria Embankment
London EC4Y 0DZ

An Hachette UK Company

1 3 5 7 9 10 8 6 4 2

A CIP catalogue record for this book
is available from the British Library.

ISBN (Mass market paperback) 978 1 4091 8104 0

ISBN (eBook) 978 1 4091 8105 7

Printed and bound in Great Britain by Clays Ltd, Elcograf S.p.A.

MIX
Paper from
responsible sources
FSC
www.fsc.org   FSC® C104740

www.orionbooks.co.uk

Contents

Introduction

I see you all around me
I hear you through the trees,
You're there within an instant
When you recognise my pleas.

Angels are beings of love to help us with all aspects of our lives, and since I began communicating with them from the age of three, I have been on a journey of recognition that has shown me how different angels can be called upon for different roles. Angels help us when we're in need, when we are in danger or struggling to make decisions. They help attract solutions, support and opportunities in a whole array of situations that we can find ourselves in throughout our lives.

They are there with us for life. The more we communicate with them, build a rapport and a relationship with them, the more we allow them to help and guide us.

Angels are messengers of God, or Source, the creator of all things. Angels of love are there to help us with self-love and relationships of all kinds, including those with our family, friends and partners. They can be called on during times of challenge, to help us communicate with others and decide if a relationship is good for us, or simply to help bring the right people and loved ones into our lives when we need them.

When we start to talk to our angels of love, we open our world to unlimited help, support, protection and learning that we couldn't possibly achieve on our own. Their love is unconditional and limitless. It is simply our perception of what we can receive from them that alters the reality of what we can actually create with their assistance. The more we develop our relationship with them, the more we learn how to bring love into our lives in all ways.

Love is the glue that binds us

Love is the glue that binds us all together as a species, as we are born with a pre-set programme in every cell of our bodies to learn how to become our best selves. This is what encourages us to preserve and enhance ourselves as humans and, in turn, attract those who help us to achieve that. Much like our fellow creatures in the animal kingdom, we're designed to procreate to continue our existence, but setting us apart from them is our added ability to learn so much about ourselves through relationships. It is through our interactions with others that we're encouraged to learn life lessons, attract better relationships and achieve our desires.

Love creates a huge array of emotions, many of which are positive, such as joy, bliss, passion, excitement, elation, contentment and peace, but at the other end of the spectrum, love can also create fear, uncertainty, jealousy, rage, grief and so on. Love is the most expansive thing we can ever possibly experience, and by allowing ourselves to embrace it and learn how to maximise its potential, we can become better human beings, living fully in this world rather than teetering on the perimeter, too scared to dip our toes into the emotional waters through fear of getting hurt.

You may have experienced this yourself, or perhaps you know others who seem to move through life untouched by drama, who live each day slowly and with safety in mind, as though it were more or less the same as any other, rather than taking risks and being challenged. You may recognise in yourself or in others the whole eclectic palette of emotions that love can create when challenged by life, having taken risks, failed, picked yourself up and found a way through, sometimes only to find yourself hitting yet more challenge.

Love is a risk. It can be pure bliss or hell, but that all depends on whether self-love has been a priority for you. Our angels of love are there to teach us about self-love, acceptance, non-judgement and opening our hearts to love all of mankind, as if they were our children, our siblings or our parents. Angels of love are there to help us learn how, when we fully love ourselves, we can attract those beneficial relationships and, in doing so, create a better world for us all to live in.

Angels of love in history

Cupids have been depicted as symbols of love throughout history. There are many variations of the story of Cupid, but in Roman mythology he was the son of Venus, the goddess of love. According to legend, Venus became jealous of Psyche's beauty and was angry when Cupid fell in love with the mortal girl and married her. Psyche was never allowed to look at him and so he visited her only at night, when it was dark.

Despite Cupid's warning, Psyche's sisters persuaded her to look at him, so on one of his nightly visits, she glanced at him and he left her, enraged. Wandering aimlessly, she came upon Venus, who wanted to destroy her, and so she gave her challenges, each one more difficult than the last. Eventually Psyche was ordered to deliver a box to the underworld and collect some of the beauty of Proserpina. Psyche was warned not to open the box, but inquisitiveness got the better of her. She looked, and found nothing but deadly slumber inside, which caused her to fall into a deadly sleep.

Cupid, however, still loved her, and when he found her he was able to put the deadly sleep back into the box. Psyche was made into a goddess and the gods gathered to celebrate their wedding with a lavish feast. This is where 'and they all lived happily ever after' is said to have come from.

The classical Roman figure of Cupid had evolved from the Ancient Greek god Eros, and many temples and cults were dedicated to worshiping this god of love. He was depicted as the chubby cherub that we know today, who shot arrows from his bow at intended targets, and was characteristically blindfolded (as love was said to be 'blind').

Ancient Rome also celebrated fertility and the coming of spring with Lupercalia, one of its oldest traditional festivals. It was a matchmaking ritual whereby young women would place their name in an urn and eligible bachelors would draw a name from it and spend the rest of the festival with the young women they had chosen. As Christianity became more prominent in Rome, Pope Gelasius abolished this ritual and replaced it with something more spiritual, so that instead of girls' names, bachelors would pull out the name of a saint, so that they could learn all about the attributes of that saint throughout the year ahead and become more 'saintly' — and this included St Valentine.

At the time, Gelasius had declared a celebration of St Valentine, the patron saint of lovers, to be held on 14 February every year, which was the day he was executed. Legend has it that Valentine had been a priest and had disobeyed the Emperor Claudius by conducting wedding ceremonies for men whom the emperor had earmarked for military service. He was taken prisoner and, while in prison, he fell in love with a young girl who visited him.

Before he was executed, he wrote the girl a letter signed 'from your Valentine', which went on to create the romantic tradition that we know of today.

During the Renaissance, between the fifteenth and seventeenth centuries, when the likes of Leonardo da Vinci,

Michelangelo and Raphael were producing incredible paintings and sculptures, artists were exploring the subject of love through their art and creating characters known as '*putti*': male babies or toddlers that represented pure love. Often, they had angel wings and eventually artists started depicting Cupid with the wings of an angel, too.

People then began to refer to these as 'cherubs' and saw them as representations of the 'glorious feeling of being loved'. In the Bible it is said that cherubim performed the task of protecting the Garden of Eden. So, we can see that angels of love have been passed down throughout history to remind us of their vital role within humanity.

About me

Up to the age of three, I remember nothing but love and security. My family were always happy, and laughter was a constant in our home. However, one day that all changed when I was taken to live with my father and never returned.

From the early days in my father's home I was frightened, alone and very uncertain of what would happen to me. I learned very quickly that I would never go back to the loving environment I'd once known, and my childhood from then on was a fearful and unsafe experience until I left home at the age of seventeen. The people who had taken over as my custodians were continuously volatile and violent, and I lived every day wondering if it would be my last.

My earliest recollections of angels were during those first days in that house. The safest time for me was when everyone was asleep, and that's when I prayed to be rescued. Through my dreams I had visions of angels who would reassure me and talk to me, and I was conscious from a very young age of 'lucid dreaming' — in other words, I was aware that I was dreaming, even though I was asleep. I was able to control my dreams, often making the most of my freedom with my angels, and regularly revisiting the same dream night after night to spend time in that safe space with my newfound friends.

I would often have conversations with my angels about what I was going through, and on many occasions they would simply say, *'You are always loved, Amanda. We are always with you.'*

Over time I would come to recognise the different angels who would appear to help me depending on what my needs were. When life at home got tougher, I started to experience their loving guidance in my wakeful state as they taught me how to recognise when they were around me.

If protection was needed, I experienced warrior-like angels who reassured and calmed me through challenging times. If healing was needed, I was soothed by the gentleness of angels who cared for me until I was well again. Angels of light helped me to communicate and learn how to navigate my volatile world, and angels of love helped me to learn how to love myself and those around me, despite how they behaved towards me.

I believe that if it weren't for my angels of love, I would never have broken free of the catastrophic negative conditioning that went on to haunt me for many years into adulthood, not only in my relationship with myself, but in my relationships with others, too.

No matter what I was going through, when I was desperate, angry, frightened and alone, my angels of love would remind me, '*Amanda, remember the meaning behind your name – "worthy to be loved" – as in the future you will show others that love is ultimately all that's needed.*'

Despite how dreadfully I was treated as a child, my angels of love continually showed me how to stay true to the essence of my higher self in order not only to survive, but to learn how to love no matter what. They taught me that love conquers all. Even during my darkest moments and deepest doubts, their wisdom, guidance and unwavering love helped me to find solutions and overcome traumas, and to feel deep love throughout my childhood.

During those early years, my angels of love guided me towards positive relationships with people outside of my house who meant the world to me, so that, despite what went on at home, my life was still filled with love and support. However, as I approached the age of eighteen, my relationships started to change and became increasingly destructive.

As my teenage years unfolded after I left my childhood home, I sought freedom and an escape from the life I knew, and I shut down from my angels. In the dark moments I called out to them but couldn't hear them over the noise of my dramas, so I resigned myself to the thought that they'd abandoned me. I felt alone and confused.

As I got older, my relationships plummeted and became disastrous, causing mayhem in my life, until finally, when I was at rock bottom, in a desperate attempt to save myself from total destruction, I prayed for my angels to return.

The moment I knew they were there came the following day, when I opened a newspaper to see an article that prompted me to apply for a numerology report. Numerology is similar to astrology: when you calculate your 'life path number' by adding up your date of birth (mine is 7), it can provide vast insights into what sort of person you are, what kind of role you may play in life and how this affects your relationships.

When I received my report, I discovered what my angels were trying to tell me — that I had to make huge changes in my life if I was to survive. And so, from then on, my relationship with my angels of love started to develop once again. I was desperate to overcome the destructive patterns that I'd carried from my childhood, but also my angels reminded me that I was to show others about the power of love in the future: *'Amanda, it may not make sense to you now with all that you're going through, but in the future your life will change and you will show others how to change theirs.'*

This was what I held on to. Partly it was my own need to find peace, happiness and unconditional love, but intrigue also played a role in my desire to see how my life would pan out if I put all my trust and faith in their guidance.

By the end of my twenties I had moved away from deep isolation, fear and self-loathing. It took me many years to learn from my angels of love how to invest in my own self-worth through mindful practices. The more I invested, the more I saw my world change and my relationships with others started to change too, as I again began to attract into my life those who would serve my highest good.

As people around me started to see my transformation, they approached me to help them make changes for themselves. Given that I felt I still had such a long way to go, I was nervous of how I could possibly help others, but whenever I wanted to hide away, my angels of love would remind me: *'Don't shrink away through fear of failure; trust that we will guide you to help those who reach out, as you are more ready than you realise.'*

Slowly but surely, as each person approached me for guidance, I trusted and opened up to allow my angels of love to share with me what would help them on their own journeys. As people then began to experience their own positive changes, my trust in my angels' guidance built and so I continued to invest in my own personal growth.

Looking back at my life as a young adult, I can see that I've changed unrecognisably, having finally come to love myself once more, just as I did as a child. My angels of love taught me that without self-love I couldn't possibly expect to attract loving relationships, and despite experiencing times of great stubbornness and resistance towards their guidance, today I'm incredibly grateful for the life I've created because of their patience, love and understanding.

Every day I call upon my angels for help and guidance in a variety of situations — my angels of love most of all. They help me with my practices for self-love and my relationship with myself, as well as my relationships with others. As our lifelong experiences are shaped by the people we come into contact with every day, we all have a choice in how we deal with them. I learned from a very young age how to cope with adversity and make the very best of difficult situations, but more than that, I learned that I am never alone and always loved. With unwavering faith that my angels will help me no matter what, I know I can always deal with whatever life throws at me.

Who this book is for

This book is for those who may feel isolated, alone or disconnected at times and want to find a deeper meaning to their life. It is for anyone who may have had relationship difficulties with themselves or others, suffered addictions, negative behaviours, repeated cycles or patterns that are destructive or those who just want life to become more joyful, exciting or adventurous. It's for those who already have an understanding that angels touch their lives and want to deepen that relationship, or those who would like to open up to their angels of love for the first time in order to improve all their relationships. Ultimately, it is for those who seek inner and outer peace.

Our angels of love are there to guide us in all aspects of our relationships; they can help us find happiness, and enable us to share joy with others and overcome the darker aspects of our lives, encouraging us to grow and achieve our desires.

When we allow our angels of love to assist us, it enables us to see the enormous capabilities we have as humans to live a harmonious life, while empowering us to overcome the many challenges life throws our way, which has an equally positive effect on those around us. Even people we never meet will feel the benefits, as we are all connected intrinsically by an energy force that binds us as a species.

When we struggle alone in the world and rely on limited beliefs, we create an incomplete reality of the life we can make for ourselves. When we embrace our divinity and open ourselves to the help that is constantly being offered to us by our angels of love, we can start to remove the toxicity from our lives and build positive foundations from a place of empowerment, and connect to the 'bigger picture'.

If you've ever contemplated or seen signs that there is far more going on than just the reality of the physical world, then you are in good company, as millions of others have had similar experiences. All of us have the ability to see this, but only some of us *choose* to explore it. Once you welcome and develop your relationship with your own angels of love you will start to see your reality change as solutions and opportunities appear, dramas lessen, healing takes place, your senses heighten, your mindset broadens and your everyday reality transforms.

My angels are my first port of call when I need them. They're a listening ear, my solution-finding experts, my allies, my best friends and my support system. Through their guidance, I have found the essence of my innate self, my authenticity, my truth and my power. I have found my ability to overcome adversity and find peace, and above all I have built trust that no matter what life throws at me, my angels of love are always close by to help me not only deal with it, but also learn lessons and take the positives from the situation.

At one time in my life it was all high drama. I felt like I was in a washing-machine cycle, being thrown around by life, and only when the programme stopped would I feel the relief. Unfortunately, I was exhausted by each experience, and while recovering, more often than not I would find myself thrust into yet another drama with little or no energy left to deal with it. Each cycle depleted my energy more and more, until finally my physical body could take no more and I became seriously ill.

Today I recognise challenges before they become dramas and my angels of love guide me peacefully around them, as if I'm navigating a small boat around an obstacle in a river; now, I can gently float past and continue on my journey.

I want you to develop the same relationship with your own angels of love and to believe that they are constantly by your side through the good times and, more importantly, through the times of challenge. It will help make this world a better place for us *all* to live in.

13

Regardless of our childhood experiences or the challenges life has thrown at us as adults, no matter what our cultural or religious beliefs, or our nationality or race, our angels are there to guide, love and protect us. We're all designed to become our best self, to allow ourselves to become more in tune with life and therefore discover our truth and find the right path. When we pay attention, we find our peace and our place in this world, our people and our purpose. Angels of love ultimately help us fulfil our potential for the highest good of all.

How to use this book

This book is designed to be read again and again so that you can draw on it throughout your life, whenever you need it most. We live in a fast-paced world as it is, so this book is intended to help you take your foot off the accelerator long enough for you to listen and pay attention to your angel communication. For me, spirituality is not about spending hours taking part in rituals that just add to your busyness and stress, so I have incorporated the following practical elements into this book, which will enhance your angelic communication.

Your light bulb moment
Do you remember the simple electricity circuits we used to make in science classes at school, when the light bulb would

not shine if there were any tiny holes or 'faults' in the circuit? Consider this simple experiment as an analogy of your own spiritual awakening. If you are carrying any fears, underlying assumptions, external obstacles or negative memories, they will create 'faults' in your own personal energy circuit and will stop you from receiving loving blessings from your angels. Throughout this book you will find activities that are designed to free your personal energy circuit of any 'faults' so that your angels can actively shine their light on your journey. These activities are called **Your light bulb moment** because I hope they will inspire you and enhance the line of communication between you and your angels of love.

Meditations

Meditation has its origins in the East and helps to still the mind and allow you to reach a heightened level of awareness. There are many studies that show meditation to have a huge beneficial effect on the mind and body.

Meditation is an incredibly healing practice. Mental nutrition is necessary for self-improvement; it aligns us and brings about a sense of 'wholeness'. Quieting the internal chatter and shedding the outer irritating clutter in our life is far more important than you may realise. Meditation has an exceptional way of 'turning down and tuning out' the noise pollution, and many people who fill their lives with sound to blot out stress find that once they incorporate meditation, their wellbeing shifts radically and often their lifestyles and relationships change, too, to match their new, lighter vibration.

Some of the benefits of meditation include stress reduction, fewer signs of ageing, an appreciation for life, a sense of having more time and improved brain function. It helps you sleep well and feel connected, and improves your metabolism. It also boosts immunity and fights diseases, increases your attention span and helps with pain relief. Think of meditation as opening a metaphysical door from the physical world into the energy world every time you want to communicate with your angels.

Affirmations

Throughout the book affirmations are included for you to use and incorporate into your daily life in order to create a mindset that is more in alignment with the high vibration of your angels of love. Simply put, affirmations are positive statements in the present tense that you read to yourself to assert your desires in the future, as if they are your reality now.

Angels of love respond to your positive statements and therefore deliver your requests in the form that serves your highest good. You can select and use these affirmations as part of your daily ritual. The best time to read them is first thing in the morning as you wake or last thing at night before you sleep. Angels love us to create ritual, so choose what works best for you.

Count your blessings

These notes pages at the end of each chapter provide an opportunity for you to reflect on the many positive things your angels of love are doing for you. They do a lot of things to help you, so it's always worth making time to express your gratitude and thank them for the big and little things as often as possible. Counting your blessings and being grateful for what you have in life shows the Universe that you appreciate its help and are worthy of receiving it.

A few things you might want to collect before reading this book

Pen and paper

In my experience, often some of my best angelic communications occur at the times when I'm most compromised. I can be in the shower in the morning when a solution that I've been struggling to find will suddenly come to me from the angels, which really makes me chuckle. I used to wait until I had finished my shower (or whatever else I was in the middle of doing), in the hope that I would remember their message later. However, nine times out of ten, my mind would soon fill with other things I needed to do in my day and then I'd forget what they'd tried to tell me. Nowadays, I make sure that I am never far from a pen and some paper so I can record my angels' golden nuggets of insight, and I suggest you do the same so you can get the most out of this book and from their help.

Talismans

Lucky objects such as horseshoes, rabbits' feet or charms that are thought to have magic powers have been used for thousands of years to enhance angelic communication. It doesn't matter if your talisman is a pair of lucky old socks, a beloved cuddly toy or a photograph of someone special — it's only important that it is considered lucky to you.

Candles
Candles are commonly used for ceremonies, meditation, prayer and angel connection. Often candles are lit during prayer to bring about positive changes or hope in trying situations.

Crystals
Crystals are used to converse with angels of love as they radiate a tiny charge of piezoelectricity, and when placed in our energy field that charge acts like a transducer, transforming one form of energy to another. As crystals are created in the earth and contain the highest blueprint of nature, they contain the vibration of unconditional love. Therefore, when we come into contact with them, depending on what their particular properties contain, they can help us to transform our negative vibrations into positive ones, therefore transforming our negative programming into positive.

Enjoy the journey

This book will guide you through the steps of talking with your angels of love and will enable you to smoothly integrate spiritual changes into today's modern world. Absorb this book, embrace the tools I give you and take my advice into your heart. I only ask that you be open to the whole process and trust me if I push you into uncharted emotional territories. We can't expect change for the better if we only want to do the nice things and avoid the difficult. Being open to your angels of love will take courage, a curious mind, a warm heart and a promise to stop judging yourself along the way.

1

What Is Love?

Love cannot be captured
Nurtured it will bloom,
Its truth and grace will guide you home
To the sound of your own tune.

Love is an energy that is expansive, limitless and timeless. Love can be shared but not bought or sold. Love can be given but not taken, and while we think we can control and manipulate love at times, because of the very nature of its creation, we cannot. Surrendering to the true essence of love is the only way to fully understand and work within the realms of its laws.

Throughout our lifetime we will experience a multitude of loves. Love for our family, our friends, our neighbours, our colleagues. We'll experience love for our partners, our pets, our hobbies and the mementoes of loving relationships that we collect or are given. We will love our community, where we live and the places we visit, and alongside all of this, ultimately, we're wired to love our planet and all who reside on her.

Love comes in all shapes and forms. We can feel instant love for someone or something that fires a connection within our heart, and likewise we can lose it in a heartbeat if we feel betrayed, hurt or threatened in some way.

Love is complex, diverse and multifaceted, and we must undertake a lifelong lesson in mastery and wisdom, not to conquer it, but to learn how to surrender to its magnificence.

Symbols of love

The heart

The heart has been associated with love ever since the Ancient Greeks, through poets such as Sappho, who lived on the island of Lesbos during the seventh century BC and wrote about her '*mad heart quaking with love*'. It is said that she lived surrounded by female disciples and wrote passionate poems of love for them. Plato also claimed that the heart played the central part in love and emotions, while Aristotle went on to argue that it held the greatest power over all our anatomy.

And while the anatomical heart looks nothing like it, the oldest known symbol of the heart is the one we've come to recognise today throughout society, on cards and in books, art and emojis. The first known recorded symbol of the heart shape was discovered on a coin from the Ancient Roman city of Cyrene and dates from around 490 BC. The coin bore the image of a silphium plant (a now-extinct species of giant fennel), which had a seed pod that resembled a heart shape. Silphium was a huge part of the rich trade of this North African economy; it was used as a seasoning, for medicinal purposes, as a perfume and also as an aphrodisiac.

Wedding rings

Likewise, the symbolism of the wedding ring on the bride's fourth finger dates back to Ancient Roman times when they believed that a vein from the heart was connected to this finger; they called it *vena amoris* or the 'vein of love'. Although this notion was incorrect, the tradition was carried on into medieval times, when the church encouraged grooms to place a wedding band on the bride's fourth finger because of that vein, and continues to this day.

Roses

The rose has long been a symbol of love and romance. It is said that the tears of Aphrodite, Greek goddess of love, and the blood of Adonis, her lover, flowed into the ground and created red roses, signifying love until 'death do us part'. Roman mythology thought that red roses in particular represented love and beauty, and believed that goddesses loved to bathe with them or surround themselves with rose petals in their sleeping quarters.

Early Christians said that the flower represented the Virgin Mary's virtue, while in the Hindu religion, Lakshmi, the goddess of fortune and prosperity, is said to have been created from 1008 red rose petals and 108 large roses as a bride for Vishnu. Hindus, therefore, have always believed that roses represent romance and love.

In an ancient Arabic tale, it is said that a nightingale saw a white rose, which caused the bird to sing. As the bird came to love the rose and held its body close to it, it was pierced with a thorn through its heart, causing blood to cover the rose, turning it red.

During the Victorian era, flowers played an incredibly important part in the expression of feelings. Gifts of flowers were often given on special occasions, and different flowers were thought to convey different meanings; roses were considered to be the flowers of love.

Today flowers are still given as an expression of thanks, appreciation and love — roses especially for the latter. A single red rose is often seen to symbolise a gesture of 'I love you' in a new relationship. A dozen, however, represents 'love and appreciation', as the number twelve often relates to cycles, such as the twelve hours of the clock, the twelve months of the year or the twelve signs of the zodiac. A gift of a dozen roses when in a relationship traditionally marks an appreciation of time together and the completion of these cycles, while 100 red roses can demonstrate 'devotion' in a relationship that has grown over time.

The ankh
One of the most iconic symbols of Ancient Egyptian hiero-glyphics, the ankh means 'life'. Similar to the Christian

cross but with a loop at the top, it represents life and immortality but also fertility. There are many theories as to what the ankh represents, from a sandal (with the top representing a toe loop) to a flower, but, more in keeping with the true meaning of the symbol, it has mostly been regarded by scholars as symbolising the union of the goddess Isis with her husband Osiris, after she had resurrected him from the dead.

Swans

Both the Greek goddess of love and desire Aphrodite and her Roman counterpart Venus have been depicted with swans to suggest love. Swans mate for life, and today we often see images of swans facing one another, with their beaks touching, their long necks forming the shape of a heart to represent this.

Doves

The majority of dove species mate for life, which, like swans, means they are often thought to symbolise partnership and marriage. In Christian belief, the dove is a symbol of peace and love, with two doves together acting as a sign of faithfulness. Hindus, meanwhile, believe that doves are a symbol of the endless capacity we have in our hearts to love.

Greek and Roman mythology believed that doves were sacred to the goddess of love. Doves are often pictured with Aphrodite and Venus in art, and could also be sacrificed in their honour.

Maple leaves

In Japanese and Chinese cultures, the maple leaf is a symbol for lovers as a reminder of the beauty of love each and every day. Settlers in North America placed maple leaves at the end of their bed to ward off demons, have a peaceful sleep and to attract sexual pleasure. Likewise, a stork is thought to use maple branches to build its nest to represent fertility. Maple syrup, which is known for its sweetness, is also associated with the 'sweetness' of being in love.

The Claddagh ring

According to an old legend from an Irish village called Claddagh, a fisherman called Richard was once captured by pirates while at sea and taken to Africa as a slave for many years. His fellow captives died but Richard survived, and each day he stole a tiny amount of gold from his captors to make a ring for his beloved. When he finally returned to Ireland, he gave her the ring, as she had remained faithful to him while he was gone. Today, the Claddagh ring is traditionally worn to show that someone is 'spoken for' before marriage. The heart in the ring represents love, the crown loyalty and the hands friendship.

Love knots

These usually take the form of two pieces of rope tied together, seemingly in a figure-of-eight pattern, which has no beginning or end, symbolising eternity. It was said in the Celtic tradition that sailors would create these knots to symbolise their love for their beloveds while at sea and present them on their return. It's also believed that, back in the time of the prophet Muhammad, young Muslim women would tie such knots as a way to send messages to their lovers.

The three-leaf clover

Ireland's national symbol, the three-leaf clover has been regarded as sacred since ancient times. St Patrick declared that it represented hope, faith and love, or the Holy Trinity in Christianity, and today some still wear this symbol on their wedding day for good luck in marriage.

Shells

The Italian Renaissance artist Sandro Botticelli created the famous painting *The Birth of Venus* in the early fifteenth century, in which Venus, the Roman goddess of love, is birthed from a scallop shell and brought to shore. Shells are seen as 'protectors of love', just as they protect pearls, and appear in many cultures, including those of the Ancient Romans, Native Americans and Hindus.

Apples

Apples have been significant ever since the Bible told the story of Eve convincing Adam to eat the forbidden apple, the fruit of knowledge in the Garden of Eden, which represented temptation. In Roman mythology, meanwhile, Venus, the goddess of love and desire, was often depicted holding an apple, which suggested the somewhat hazardous, seductive and sensual facets of love.

In the seventh century BC it was customary for couples to share an apple in a wedding ceremony to represent a 'fruitful life', while in later Celtic traditions it was thought that, as apples had a longer shelf life when stored in a cool place, they represented love lasting long after the initial throws of passion.

The harp

Throughout art history, harps are often seen with cupids and cherubs. They are mentioned in poetry and music, too, and come from Celtic myths depicting the connection of heaven and earth through a pathway of love. In Norwegian and Icelandic cultures, on the other hand, the harp's strings were said to be like a ladder, which represented the ascension to 'higher states of love'. Harps have also been played throughout history in love songs because of the instrument's naturally gentle and flowing sound.

Jasmine

This powerfully scented flower, which originated at the foot of the Himalayas, represents love and is seen as sacred in the Hindu religion. Often Hindu goddesses wear jasmine around their necks, symbolising purity.

Archangels of love

Just as there are many symbols of love, there are also numerous specific archangels we can call upon who can help us with different aspects of love and relationships. The word 'archangel' derives from the Greek *archangelos*, which means 'chief angel'. In the Bible archangels are mentioned in the hierarchy of angels and are deemed as leaders of the other angels. I often call upon certain archangels to help me with specific situations, as their role is always to heal. The following archangels can help with love and relationships in times of challenge:

Archangel Michael

This archangel isn't typically associated with love and relationships, as he's deemed a warrior angel. He's often called upon for those who work in healing or to protect those in times of need. However, often self-doubt and fear can hold you back when making life decisions, and Michael is the perfect archangel to help you find the courage and strength you need to face these situations. It is not that fear will disappear, but Archangel Michael will help you see the purpose of your situation and guide you to the right solutions, therefore helping you to grow spiritually, mentally and emotionally.

Archangel Raguel

This archangel helps when relationships break down and there are misunderstandings or arguments. Call upon this archangel to smooth things over, create clarity and find harmony within your relationships, as Raguel helps with forgiveness and fixing rifts, even in the direst of situations.

Raguel can also be called upon if you're looking for the right partner, so if you recognise a pattern of destructive relationships in your past, this archangel can help attract the best person for your highest good.

Archangel Raphael

This archangel's name comes from the Hebrew word for 'God heals the soul'. This is the healing archangel and they can be called upon to soothe heartache. Archangel Raphael can help you heal past hurt, allowing you to move on to new relationships without being weighed down with the burden of that pain. Carrying emotional baggage, resentment or regret can block you from moving into healthy relationships in the future, so calling upon this archangel can be hugely beneficial, clearing all the negative chords that hold you back and encouraging you to move into a new relationship with confidence, self-belief and a feeling of peace with yourself and the world. This archangel can also help to heal any addictions or overindulgences that may have come about to fill the void when relationships have caused pain, helping you emotionally, mentally and physically.

Archangel Gabriel

This archangel is mentioned in the Bible as the 'master communicator' and is usually depicted holding a trumpet. She is apparently the only female archangel. She governs all forms of messages, and as good communication is one of the most important elements in a healthy relationship, she can be called upon to help when you are finding it difficult to overcome miscommunications, arguments and disputes in your relationship, and when you don't know quite what to say to your partner or loved one. I have worked with this archangel for many years, as she helps teachers, writers, artists and creatives; in fact, anyone who has a message to convey. Calling upon this archangel in times of need to help tell someone what they need to hear will create greater bonds of trust and empathy between you.

Archangel Chamuel

This is the archangel to call upon to overcome adversities and create peaceful relationships. If you have low self-esteem or experience challenges in a relationship then Chamuel can help protect you against these negative energies. When in doubt, or if needed, this archangel can help you find your personal power and the courage to deal with hardships. Chamuel helps when relationships are going through difficulties, so you can call upon this archangel to guide you to find the right solutions. Ultimately, Chamuel helps with finding lost aspects of yourself, so if there is something missing in your life, if you are seeking your purpose in this world and you want to find good friendships or a new partner, then Chamuel is always ready to be called upon.

Faith, science and language

What sets us apart from the animal and earth kingdoms is how faith, science and language shape how we react to and emanate love.

Faith

Faith has been passed on through religion and cultural practices in order to provide us with a moral and ethical compass. Faith is not just something we find through religion; it permeates various aspects of life, including human rights, conflict prevention and peace making, anti corruption, business ethics and values — all of which connect us socially as human beings. Love is the underlying energy that faith is built on.

Science

Scientific studies have shown that oxytocin, produced by the pituitary gland in the brain, is released when a person feels love. This is known as the 'cuddle' or 'love' hormone as it helps us to bond with one another.

Love also fires up the neurotransmitter dopamine, stimulating the pleasure centres of the brain. Serotonin levels are supposed to drop as well, which can lead to all sorts of emotions related to infatuation at the beginning of a new relationship. Some say that the moon is like love, which has a whole spectrum of phases.

Science has crossed into areas such as meditation, too. Over fifty scientific studies conducted over the past quarter of a century have verified the wide-ranging benefits to a nation produced by what is termed the 'Maharishi Effect'. It was discovered that in cities and towns all over the world where as little as 1 per cent of the population practised the 'Transcendental' meditation technique, there was a reversal in the crime rate and an increase in order and harmony in those populations.

It is now understood that the principles of individual consciousness affect collective consciousness as well; in other words, what we think and feel as individuals can have a profound effect on those around us. Furthermore, the studies showed that internal coherence and harmony generate an influence that extends beyond borders, which can therefore improve international relations and conflicts. So, thoughts and feelings really do have an impact on the world around us, not just on the people we come into contact with.

Language

We know how thoughts and words can have a positive or negative effect on us and the people around us, but the language we speak can have a huge impact on plants, animals and ultimately our planet as well. We can see how plants are affected over periods of time when words of hatred are repeatedly said to one plant and equally words of love are said to another through polygraph testing. The plant that has been subjected to negativity will more often than not perish, while the plant that has been nurtured through loving words will thrive.

Émile Coué was born in 1857 and found he had a great aptitude for science in school. He studied chemistry and then opened a pharmacy. He had a fascination with hypnotism and started to practise on customers who came into his pharmacy. During that time, he saw that many of his patients weren't completely hypnotised, but still seemed to be improving beyond the power of the drugs.

He decided to stop the traditional hypnosis method and created another in which he invited his patients to suggest their own healing – a process that he called 'autosuggestion'. As the success rate increased dramatically, so did his practice. He was so successful – he saw as many as 15,000 people a year – that Charles Baudouin, a well-known psychologist, wrote about him in his book *Suggestion and Autosuggestion* (1920), which was dedicated to Coué. In 1921, Dr Monier-Williams, a British physician, studied what Coué had done with his patients and opened a successful practice in London, sharing his work. Coué toured America and word spread of this amazing phenomenon. Today, it is famously known through his phrase, *'Every day in every way, I'm getting better, better and better.'*

Today this method is referred to as 'affirmation', whereby a person repeats positive statements in the present tense first thing in the morning and last thing at night to create positive changes that they desire. This has a profound positive effect not only on how we communicate ourselves, improving our vocabulary and becoming more mindful of what we say and how we think, but also on those we communicate with. Positivity is connected to the right hemisphere of our brain, to consciousness and our higher self. Our angels of love encourage us to seek positivity and, likewise, when we resonate on that higher vibration, we're best able to communicate with our angels of love. Like attracts like, and once we start working with that mindset, love attracts love.

The philosophy of love

Trying to explain what love is covers many theories and the role that it plays. If you tried to explain it to someone who's never experienced love, it would be almost impossible because of the magnitude of its parameters and its limitless expressions. There are psychological theories explaining that love, on the whole, is healthy. There are evolutionary theories that argue that it contributes towards our natural selection process. And then there are spiritual theories that suggest it is a gift from God, Source or the Divine (depending on which terminology or faith you may believe in).

Some great philosophers of love

Søren Kierkegaard (1813–1855)

Kierkegaard was a Danish existentialist philosopher, theologian, poet, religious author and social critic. He fell deeply in love with Regine Olsen, who was also deeply in love with him, and proposed to her but broke off the engagement a month later. While she threatened suicide over the break-up, he felt he could not be a true husband, writer and Christian all together. Although he was distraught, he let her go, and despite always regretting his decision, the love he had for her influenced his writing for the rest of his life.

> '*If you marry, you will regret it; if you do not marry, you will also regret it; if you marry or do not marry, you will regret both . . .*'
>
>   — *Either/Or: A Fragment of Life* (1843)

Friedrich Nietzsche (1844–1900)

Friedrich Nietzsche was a German composer, poet and cultural critic. He was a philologist and scholar, and had a huge influence on the world of philosophy. Despite proposing to Lou Salomé three times, a woman he was deeply in love with, she rebuffed him. He claimed that the only noteworthy philosopher who ever successfully married was Socrates, suggesting that marriage was beyond the intellect of men such as himself. In his controversially sexist book *Human, All Too Human* (1878) he argues that serial marriage would benefit men and domestic life would benefit women.

> '*It is not a lack of love, but a lack of friendship that makes unhappy marriages.*'
>
>   — *Beyond Good and Evil* (1886)

Bertrand Russell (1872–1970)

The 3rd Earl Russell was a British philosopher but also a mathematician, historian, writer, political activist and Nobel Laureate. He was one of the founders of analytical philosophy, and among his many brilliant achievements he was awarded the Nobel Prize in Literature for his contribution towards humanitarian principles and freedom of thought.

With liberal views on modern love, he shocked readers with his ideas about gay rights in his 1929 book *Marriage and Morals*, and though he married four times and had copious affairs during his first marriage, he claimed marriage to be an excellent institution. He did, however, feel it was too Victorian and became an avid supporter of free love, gay rights and freedom of thought until his death in 1970.

> *'To fear love is to fear life, and those who fear life are already three parts dead.'*
>
> – *Marriage and Morals* (1929)

Jean-Paul Sartre (1905–1980)

Jean-Paul Sartre was a French philosopher, political activist and a writer specialising as a playwright, novelist, biographer and literary critic. He was well known for his philosophy in existentialism. He spent his life with his partner Simone de Beauvoir, although they had a very open relationship and he became renowned for his affairs with his much younger protégés. Even though Simone and Jean-Paul never married, it was well known how much he felt for the woman he loved the longest, Simone.

> *'You know, it's quite a job starting to love somebody. You have to have energy, generosity, blindness. There is even a moment, in the very beginning, when you have to jump across a precipice: if you think about it you don't do it.'*
>
> — *Nausea* (1938)

A. J. Ayer (1910–1989)

Sir Alfred Jules Ayer (known as Freddie) was a British philosopher who was known for his expertise in logical positivism. He studied at Eton and the University of Oxford and went on to study his specialism at the University of Vienna. He was married four times during his lifetime to three different women; he was heartbroken by the death of his third wife so remarried the second. Despite his betrothals, he had numerous affairs and an illegitimate daughter, but he held strong beliefs about romantic behaviour.

> *'Even logical positivists are capable of love.'*
>
> — Quoted by A. J. Ayer in *Profiles* by Kenneth Tynan (1989 edition)

bell hooks (1952–)

bell, a professor, author, feminist and social activist, has focused her writing on oppression and class domination throughout society. During her career she's published over thirty books and numerous articles, has appeared in documentaries and taken part in public lectures addressing race, class, sexuality and feminism. From her own experience with relationship break-ups she was inspired to write about love. In *All About Love: New Visions* (2000) she introduced her ideas on how to improve modern thinking about love and how to overcome the obstacles that hinder it. She shares her thoughts on how men and women think differently, which can affect how they approach love, and raises the issue of the power struggle between the sexes and how love can't survive while this exists. Her book introduces a more spiritual look at love and explores how personal growth ultimately contributes to loving relationships.

> *'The fear of being alone, or of being unloved, had caused women of all races to passively accept sexism and sexist oppression.'*
>
> *— Ain't I a Woman* (1981)

There are many who've tried to fathom, unravel, express and compartmentalise the expansiveness of love throughout history, but there is still much to explore today.

I met Polly when she started to come to my development classes in the area I lived at the time. She was a loving and gentle soul, but she had an air of grief and sadness that emanated from her whenever I saw her. Though she was fun-loving, her life was filled with challenging relationships.

She was unhappily married to a man she cared for very much, but she had met the love of her life a few years before, who was also married. She couldn't avoid how she felt no matter how hard she tried. She also had difficulties with family members, and with few people in her life whom she could call friends, she seemed to have no one to turn to.

She was still grieving for the loss of her horse that had sadly died some years before, and while horses were her love and life, she couldn't bring herself to ever ride again. She was in debt, financially tied to her husband, bullied at work by a co-worker and felt unsupported by the management at work, who wanted to sweep the bullying under the carpet. Ironically, her employers were also bullying her into leaving in order to bring the matter to a close.

Polly met me when she was at her lowest ebb and through our classes I encouraged her to call upon her angels of love to help find solutions and bring peace into her life so that she might find the happiness and love she deserved.

Polly started to learn meditation in order to relax and become more receptive to the vibrations of her angels, and I then encouraged her to ask her angels to help with *all* her challenges while she was in a meditative state.

At first her frustration got the better of her. She was in a very desperate state indeed, but I reassured her that angels always honour our prayers when we are patient and the time is right. I called upon all the archangels to help with protection, healing, communication and forgiveness, and above all to bring unconditional love to Polly.

Over the course of a year Polly's whole world transformed. Firstly, she worked with her husband to find a solution to their debt problem, which they overcame in a matter of months. She then found the courage to speak to him in a loving way about her feelings. Even her relationship with her family started to improve, to the point where they started to build new foundations again.

Because of her love of horses, she was inspired to do an equine holistic healing course and not only passed both modules but excelled in them. The course gave her back her belief that she could ride horses once again and move on from her grief and loss. She realised she could put her energy into healing horses and, in turn, help other owners spiritually when their horses were sick or injured. Polly turned her grief into empathy in order to help others.

In the end, she divorced her husband amicably and moved to a picturesque spot in Glastonbury where she started a new life and made new friends. And the love of her life finally found the courage to leave his wife in a loving way and together he and Polly started to build a life together based on firm foundations.

Polly had changed almost every aspect of her life, despite many times feeling as though she wanted to abandon her dreams and suppress the feelings she had for her true love. Polly has kept in touch with me and is an incredible example of how we can find healing, the right relationships and a life we love to live no matter what, when we call upon our angels of love.

A prayer for guidance, love and protection

The following is a prayer for when you need to call upon your angels of love to help you in times of uncertainty or with lower-level vibrational thoughts and emotions caused by self-doubt, uncertainty or challenges within your relationships. You can use this prayer at any time, but it's an ideal prayer to say last thing at night as you sit up in bed, just before you go to sleep. You can also use this to pray for loved ones if you wish.

You can copy out this prayer and keep it by your bedside to help you through particularly challenging days and to transmute the negative aspects of your life. Angels only want the best for you and are always there to help you, but you have to ask. This prayer not only touches on aspects of your life that you might wish to change now, but also covers challenges or hardships that you may need help with in the future. By calling upon your angels of love, trust that they will help you and then watch for synchronistic signs (meaningful coincidences) over the next seventy-two hours to show that they have heard your prayers.

Breathe in for the count of four and out for the count of four for about a minute so that you are relaxed and open to the consciousness of your angels.

Dear angels of love who guide, love and protect me,
I call upon you to hear my prayers.
Through uncertainty, help guide me towards trust.

Through fear, help me to be courageous.

Through indecisiveness, help guide me resolution.

Through difficulties in relationships, help me find clarity.

Through self-doubt, help me find self-assurance and my truth.

Through self-loathing, help me find self-love and appreciation.

Through times of isolation or loneliness, help me find my people and place in this world.

Through times of frustration, help me find solutions and serenity.

Through times of sadness, help me find joy and happiness.

Through times of grief, help me find peace.

Through times of anxiety or depression, may I find contentedness and certainty.

Through times of despair, help me find hope.

Through times of envy, may I find good will.

Through times of shame, may I find self-respect and honour.

Through times of guilt, may I find fulfilment.

Through times of anger, may I find calm.

Through times of heartache, may I find comfort.

Through times of betrayal, may I find faithfulness.

Through times of rejection, may I find acceptance.

Through times of tragedy, may I find blessings.

Through times of unworthiness, may I find compassion.

May I always recognise your love, good grace and
guidance to find the highest vibration of my truth, if it be
for the highest good of all, with love and gratitude.

Amen

Your light bulb moment

Write a list of all the things that are negative, challenging or out of balance with your relationships, identifying any damaging habits or behaviours and any toxic energy, in order to start making the necessary changes to encourage self-love and loving relationships. (You may only want to work on a few points to start with, but keep the list and go back to it when you feel ready.)

Find somewhere tranquil to sit and deepen your breathing by counting to four on the in-breath and to four on the out-breath for about a minute. Then, taking one challenge at a time, ask your angels of love for guidance:

1. Ask your angels of love, what is going on for me right now? Ask them how the person or situation in question is affecting you.

2. Ask your angels of love, what am I going to do about it? Ask whether you need to take action or non-action. (Sometimes, just acknowledgement is good enough to take back your power.)

3. Look at the situation and ask your angels how you can put yourself first by being selfless but not selfish.

Once you have gone through each situation, you will start to feel yourself taking power back with the guidance of your angels of love. Remember, often it is about addressing situations when the time is right. If you need to address the person or situation to make positive changes, use loving disallowance, i.e. say no to unfair treatment or behaviour from others, but in a kind and loving way. If you need to talk to them, then speak honestly about how you feel. If it's a repeated pattern, then you may need to be mindful that you should keep up the new behaviour in order to change the outcome from negative to positive. This can bring instant results in some cases, whereas other situations can take time, but be patient, put yourself first, be loving to all people concerned and, above all, trust that you have the power to change the situations for the highest good of all when you have guidance from your angels of love.

Chapter summary

Love is expansive and limitless; it touches us spiritually, mentally, emotionally and physically. Through the millennia, man has tried to explore its many complexities through science, religion, cultural beliefs and the way in which we communicate. Through philosophy, many have tried to interpret the effect love has on us as human beings, but it is clear that each and every one of us spends our whole life learning about and experiencing aspects of love that we often can't foresee. We can call upon our angels of love to guide us through the complexities of love and upon specific archangels who can help us with particular issues in self-love and relationships.

COUNT YOUR BLESSINGS

Why do you feel blessed today . . .?

....
....
....
....
....
....
....
....
....
....
....
....
....
....
....
....
....
....

2

Self-love

Love is pure surrender,
It's limitless and free,
You taught me of its might and force
To heal and rescue me.

Self-love is the 'regard for one's wellbeing and happiness', according to the dictionary. It's not just a way of pampering yourself, however, but more an appreciation of how positive practices that support your mental, emotional, spiritual and physical self can help you grow as a human being. As you mature through self-love, you become more accepting and appreciative of your whole self, flaws and all. This allows you to go into a state of peace within yourself as you find meaning and authenticity in your life, when your personal power and purpose are able to shine through.

Ultimately, you create a fulfilling existence for yourself, which in turn attracts you to the right people who will support your own personal commitment to your self-worth.

Your inner world is a direct reflection of your outer world, so if you want to attract truly loving experiences with people who resonate with your highest ideals then this is the starting point, which often invokes a healing process. Ultimately, self-love is the root of all love.

When I finally realised I was in a loveless marriage, it took me greatly by surprise to find that it was not my marriage, nor my husband, that was at fault, but that I had little love for myself. I'd assumed up to that point that I had been unlucky in life and that it was my parents' fault or my husband's, or that it was needy friends who were causing continual unhappiness in my life. I felt that perhaps it was just my lot and that I was destined to attract negative experiences. I had no concept up until that point that I was simply carrying destructive habits and behaviours around with me that had been imprinted onto the software of my brain and that I could actually do something to change that.

Apart from my children, whom I loved unconditionally, I had very few 'true' friendships, and despite being part of a family, I felt alone and unbearably unhappy with my life. So one day my angels of love encouraged me to go to the 'self-help' section of a local bookshop and, despite having no idea what to look for, Louise Hay's *You Can Heal Your Life* almost fell off the shelf in front of me, as if trying to get my attention. I knew as soon as I read the blurb that it was for me, although I wasn't prepared for the messages the book would convey in order to heal me.

It was unfamiliar territory, putting my energy into self-healing, especially as I had to start taking responsibility for my 'stuff' and face my demons. At first, I rebelled, but the teaching from Louise's book reassured me that I would come through the process, heal and create a healthier, happy life for myself. There were times when I wanted to give up and go back to the blissful ignorance of my pain and suffering. Some days it seemed too unbearable. But the more I stood tall and faced my fears, the more I saw changes come about.

Although I knew I had some way to go, once I started to see the positive changes, I knew I had to discover more about what this self-development lark was all about. Not only did I start to see and feel things changing, my angels of love started to send me messages throughout the day to reassure me when times were tough. I began to realise that my angels of love had been trying to get me to see through the dark years of my young adulthood for a very long time, but I had been in too dark a place to see it.

Finally, as my feeling of self-worth grew, I started to gain the courage to initiate a divorce and, despite not knowing how on earth I would look after two young children under the age of four on my own financially, I had enough belief in my angels of love to keep investing in my self-love. The outcome was uncertain, but I knew with all my heart that my angels would guide, love and protect me, no matter what.

Throughout my personal transformation, I moved away from those who no longer served me and started to attract new friendships and loved ones. Surprisingly, though, I also attracted those who wanted me to help them with their own personal transformation process, too.

During those early days of helping others, I predominantly attracted those who wanted help with their relationships. Every story was different, but every process was the same, as my angels of love had shown me in a dream how I could help others to heal themselves through self-love. I have continued to adopt this same process ever since with all the clients I see and I am grateful every day for the loving guidance my angels of love still continue to offer me, to help myself and help others help themselves.

The law of attraction and self-love

The law of attraction is always at play. It is an invisible force, much like gravity, which in our day-to-day experiences pulls whatever we believe about ourselves towards us. This is especially the case in the people we love and those we may simply interact with. People cannot see or know what we believe about ourselves, but even if we try to create an air of control over our thoughts and feelings, we cannot override the law of attraction, as our experiences will reflect what we believe about ourselves regardless.

Because I was lacking in self-love, my life was always full of high drama throughout the early years of my life and well into adulthood. Looking back, I recognise the moment of transition when I finally asked my angels of love to help me change. We all know someone who seems to always have so many challenges, so many dramas in their life — it seems that as soon as they get over one drama, the next arrives in another form to test them. Maybe you recognise this in yourself, or in who you were in the past before self-love became part of your healthy regime.

Recognising a lack of self-love

1. You may make decisions out of guilt or a need to please others in order to avoid conflict and have difficulty setting boundaries.

2. You may find that certain people in your life sap your energy and give little back in return. Every time they're with you they seem to drain your energy and you dread communicating with them but feel obliged to.

3. Even though you have people in your life, you feel alone, isolated or misunderstood and feel worse when you're alone.

4. You constantly look at external situations or people around you and feel it's not you but what's going on in your life that is wrong.

5. You feel you've missed opportunities or had bad luck in your career and relationships.

6. You recognise that your inner dialogue is disrespectful towards an aspect of yourself that you do not like, which is repeated on a regular basis.

7. You chastise yourself for failing, judging your errors or limitations as bad, and never seem to be satisfied that you are doing your best.

8. You have toxic relationships in your life that you cannot let go of through fear.

9. You show up in front of people with a mask on in an effort to be someone you are not, through fear of revealing who you really are.

10. You find it hard to accept your story of who you are and try to change the narrative to fit the person you feel others want you to be.

11. Your relationship with your partner is based on making you feel complete, rather than feeling whole as an individual.

12. Your partner or loved one doesn't make you happy anymore and therefore you are focusing on what others are not giving you, rather than what you are not giving to yourself.

13. You perhaps engage in addictions — such as drugs, alcohol, food, toxic relationships, over-exercise or work — to fill a void in your life.

14. You feel fatigued, depressed, anxious or uncertain about your future.

15. You need others to validate your existence.

16. Your life is packed with activities that fill your day and you never seem to have enough time for you, even though you desperately need it.

17. Your health has suffered, or you've experienced burnout.

18. You judge others for their wrong choices or lifestyle, while deep down this reflects a part of yourself that you wish you could let go of.

You may feel that some or many of the statements above ring true for you. If that's the case, know that you can change when you invest in yourself and ask your angels of love to guide you to make the necessary transition, which will bring about self-healing and therefore self-love.

When twenty-eight-year-old Julie first visited me as a client, she had been journeying through one of the darkest and most challenging periods of her life. She'd been in an immensely painful place for many years, carrying unresolved childhood traumas and fears surrounding her relationship with her father and, as a result, men. Her life felt empty in all areas, including her work. She felt she was literally dying as her body had started to shut down and it looked like she might end up in a wheelchair.

She visited several specialist doctors, had copious tests and brain scans and finally was given multiple injections in her neck to help her heal. She was diagnosed with all sorts of conditions and in desperation she resorted to a holistic energy-healing session. It was then that she noticed that something life-changing was beginning to take place. She still experienced endless nightmares, day and night, as well as anxiety attacks and destructive relationships, but the results were bringing about remarkable healing in her physical body and the journey of self-realisation had begun.

She started to meditate and spend time in nature, and that's when she began to experience synchronicities that couldn't be explained with the rational mind. She also started to attract people who helped her find her way to healing and helped to release her from her constant pain. When Julie started working with me, she was open and willing to do whatever she had to do, as by then she had faith that she was on the right path. I asked what Julie needed and my angels of love said, *'Encourage Julie to call upon us to help guide her to self-love.'* Julie was ready by then, so it was a natural progression for her on her journey back to wellbeing.

Through her angels of love, Julie finally started to recognise that she was looking for love in all the wrong places, never taking the time to start rebuilding within herself. The final straw came as she felt pressure at home from family and friends to leave her last destructive relationship for the sake of her health.

Over a few months, what then took place changed her life rapidly. I worked with Julie to shift the negative programmes that no longer served her and to help her tap into her fullest potential. Each session felt like an eraser wiping out the old and bringing forth new and productive patterns of behaviour. The shifts were fast and powerful, aligning Julie strongly with her power and her inner voice so that she gained clarity and understanding of her life's purpose. She finally found the peace she'd always searched for, which brought with it better relationships, a deeper connection to who she was and a recognition of her passion for health and nutrition. She went on to study and dedicate her life to educating others about self-love and today shares her profound messages of healing and support with others through her love of writing.

The truth about self-love

1. Self-love is not selfish, but selfless. In order to give to others, you need to give to yourself first and foremost.

2. If you feed your soul, you feed your blueprint (the highest version of yourself), which creates growth.

3. It's healthy to give to yourself in a loving way that nurtures the mind, body and spirit.

4. Self-love energises you so that, in turn, you can give more to others.

5. Self-love should be a daily investment. Much like riding a bike, it's far easier to keep peddling with a little effort, rather than peddling like mad for a while and then stopping, as you have to put so much effort into getting started again.

6. Self-love gives you what the outside world can never give.

7. When you make choices from a place of self-love, you are in alignment with your higher self and therefore make good judgements and decisions.

8. When you learn to love yourself, you discover your boundaries, which speaks volumes about the value you place on yourself.

9. You attract healthy relationships that match the vibration of your higher ideals, based on the value you see in yourself.

10. Your authentic self has all the hallmarks of success and you show up every day in all situations, giving it 100 per cent.

11. You give yourself the treats you deserve as a reward. Having fun shows the Universe you are worthy and deserving.

12. Self-love enables you to be more present in your relationships with others and therefore to enjoy more fulfilling and rewarding experiences with them.

13. You are compassionate towards others, though you're discerning with what you will take from them.

14. How you care for and think about yourself shows up in others.

15. Self-love allows your authentic self to shine. When you are certain of yourself you can reach out for help when you need it.

16. Self-love allows you to say that you are enough.

17. Self-love is mental and emotional freedom.

18. Self-love gives you the ability to forgive yourself for your mistakes without judgement.

Practices that support self-love

Engaging with practices that support and stimulate self-love in a healthy and harmonious way creates a foundation from which we can explore our full potential. Here are some examples of how to encourage love into your life:

Love for the physical

- Nutrition and exercise
- Healthy sleep patterns
- Body-work, such as massage and reflexology
- Cleansing and detoxing rituals, such as saunas and treatments
- Spending time in nature
- Spending time with animals/pets
- A little retail therapy
- Decluttering your personal space at work and at home
- Hugging or holding hands with someone you love or respect
- Bringing fresh flowers into your home
- Doing something that you love each day
- Spending time with those you love

Love for the mind

- Creativity and hobbies
- Visualisation, intention and affirmations
- Prayer, forgiveness and gratitude

- Mindfulness — thoughts of self and others
- Being mindful of what you read/absorb
- Being mindful of who you spend time with
- Positive programmes and beliefs
- Uplifting music and positive environments
- Learning
- Adventure
- Coming out of your comfort zone

Love for the emotions

- Forming right relationships that feed you
- Developing your relationship with your self
- Building an awareness of what affects your feelings
- Learning to sense what your emotions are teaching you at any given moment, so you can embrace it or make a change
- Spreading kindness to others
- Giving time and energy to others
- Seeking support from others
- Avoiding toxic activities
- Laughing as often as you can
- Promoting optimistic activities in your life

Love for the spirit

- Meditation and relaxation
- Tools and talismans, such as crystals, candles and symbols
- Soul work — a personal journey of discovery

- Workshops, study, books and growth — all chosen through discernment
- Self-development
- Exploring your faith
- Journal-keeping
- Developing a clear energy field

Meditation for the heart energy centre

When I first started to meditate, I found it difficult to focus and found my mind constantly looking for ways to distract me. It would create any nonsense in order to deter me from giving myself the self-love I deserved. This meditation came to me as a way to open my heart and allow myself to be more open, loving and free in order to trust and let go. Trust is a huge part of self-love, as it allows you to become more mindful of what you choose to attract into your life, so try this meditation on a regular basis to open your heart energy centre so that you can fully engage with all of life. Only then will you discern what you want to experience, learn from and engage with, and only then will you be aware of your full potential.

You can record this meditation slowly on your phone or some other device, so that whenever you feel life is testing you and you're starting to lose trust and feel yourself retracting from life to protect yourself, you can turn to it. This meditation will help you to be open and free but still fully centred in the knowledge that your angels of love are there to guide and protect you.

Find yourself a quiet, tranquil space. Make sure you won't be distracted and perhaps have some tranquil music playing gently in the background. Light a candle and, if you can, have some rose essential oil in a burner so that the smell infuses into the room. (Rose oil boosts self-esteem, invoking confidence and mental strength, and can help with depression and anxiety, so it is a great oil to use as an antidepressant. It's also a great oil to use if you have issues with your partner or to invoke love in your life.)

Close your eyes and take a deep breath in. On the exhalation, count slowly to four. On the next in-breath count slowly to four and then out to the count of four again. Slow your breathing down and become mindful of each breath in and out, while rhythmically counting to four. Continue to breathe in and out to the count of four until you feel your body start to relax.

Focus on your breath for a couple of minutes to deepen your relaxation, taking the time to pause for as long as you feel necessary for the recording.

Know that your angels of love will guide you through this meditation and help you to open your heart to accept self-love, freedom and peace. Imagine that you're surrounded by a beautiful pink aura, much like a bubble of love, and that you are safe and protected in that rich pink light.

You may feel warmth, you may feel a tingling sensation, you may even feel parts of your body being touched or brushed lightly by an angel's feather. Sit with this imagery for a moment and allow your other senses to relay back to you what is happening right now. Each time may be different, so do not judge it . . . just sit with it and absorb whatever sensations you're experiencing right now.

When you feel that your body has become nice and relaxed, start to scan yourself from the top of your head to the tips of your toes, slowly downwards through your body, checking to see if there's any tension whatsoever. When you meet tension, anywhere in your body, just thank your angels of love for showing you and ask them to send love to that area of your body. Take a deep breath and on your in-breath imagine pink light is pouring into that area, and as you exhale, release the tension. Keep breathing that pink light into that area through as many breaths as is needed until you feel deeply relaxed and the tension has dissolved.

Continue to scan your body and breathe pink light into any areas that you feel may hold resistance.

Finally, when your body has become still, clear your mind and imagine you are sitting on your own in a tranquil garden on a bench. You can see a beautiful pink rose, which is closed but fully mature and ready to open. The rose is about a metre in front of you and stands upright and strong among a whole bed of rose bushes, but you notice this particular rose because it seems to be more beautiful than all the other roses.

The sun is shining and while you're sitting under a tall, shaded tree, the warmth of the sun's rays are shining through the branches onto your body, just enough for you to *feel energised and relaxed. You notice the peace around you, as the garden is filled with flowers, plants, bushes, trees and a small pond with a fountain, which is a feast for your eyes.*

You notice that the birds are singing – you can even hear different varieties. The water is gently pouring over stones into the pond and every now and then you hear the splashing of a fish in the calm water. There are insects skimming the surface, and you marvel at how they hover like little boats and zip effortlessly across the water, and just as you feel yourself getting absorbed in the pond life, a gentle breeze mildly caresses your face, as if you've been softly kissed by the wind.

You feel safe, tranquil and at peace, and while you sit there you allow your gaze to slowly move back to the single pink rose in front of you. You allow your gaze to gently rest upon the rose and imagine now that it is symbolically sitting in your heart energy centre. Slowly imagine now that the rose is starting to open. Petal by petal, from the outside in, the rose starts to reveal its inner beauty.

As you watch the rose unfold, you start to notice how each petal is shaped similarly but still individually created and formed, and you marvel at how perfect each one is. The petals seem to expand and grow as they reveal their glory, and as you watch them open one by one, you somehow seem to know in your heart that there are 100 petals on this particular rose, and as each unfolds, they seem to represent an aspect of yourself unfolding. You start to count slowly backwards then as each petal unfurls . . . 100, 99, 98, 97. . . (continue to count downwards until you reach the count of one) and as you finally reach the count of one, you'll see that your rose is fully formed and open, just as you have opened your heart energy centre to reveal every aspect of your beautiful, authentic, loving self.

Sit for a while and absorb the beauty and colour of that rose. Breathe in the scent and allow its rich fragrance to fill your nostrils. Imagine yourself touching that rose, feeling the soft petals with your fingers, absorbing their delicacy and texture. Finally allow yourself to become mindful of how you feel right now. Sit for a while and allow that feeling to wash over you.

When you feel ready to come back into the room, remind yourself that you can come back to your tranquil garden and visit your rose any time you want to open your heart. Slowly let your eyes open and allow the surroundings in your room to filter into your eyes. You should be feeling relaxed, peaceful, open and centred, ready to carry on with your day.

Your light bulb moment

The first time I was introduced to the concept of 'an hour of power a day', it started a habitual routine of giving self-love, which I've never failed to be mindful of since. On days when I am overwhelmed and let life take over, I notice that my health, relationships or energy levels are affected. So, being mindful of giving yourself an hour of power a day can be instrumental in setting yourself up with good daily habits that support your self-love regime and keep your momentum continually moving forward. This will support the foundations for creating the healthy relationships that you desire, but most importantly, it will reflect outwardly what you're inwardly giving to yourself, which ultimately attracts what you desire.

Your hour of power could be a yoga class, a walk in the park, a date with friends for lunch, reading a book or cycling by the river. It can be a relaxing spa treatment or even just a bath away from the family to give yourself time to rejuvenate. It could be that you just want to watch a movie, write some of that book you've been putting off or listen to music in the garden while you sit in the sun. Whatever it is, make sure it is something you are giving to yourself wholeheartedly, because it makes you happy.

If you find you only have time for half an hour or twenty minutes even to spare at any given time, then make sure you factor in another thirty or forty minutes' worth of something else for yourself that day that will give you that 'top up'.

Remember, if you procrastinate or make excuses that you don't have enough time in your hectic schedule, then this is *exactly* what you need to incorporate into your life in order to slow down and become more effectual with your daily routine. It will keep you aligned to your higher self and create a productive outcome to your day.

Try this for two weeks. Self-love will soon start to attract the positive relationships and situations that reflect how you now feel about yourself. You won't want to look back as you see your life slowing down and becoming more productive and harmonious.

Chapter summary

Self-love is the primary focus if we are to find peace, fulfilment, confidence and acceptance of all that we are. When we invest in ourselves, we discover who we really are and, above all, what we really want, as sometimes what we think we want can come from a place of misinterpretation, based on negative beliefs. Once we 'find' who we are, we are much more capable of attracting loving relationships and situations that ultimately support our higher ideals and highest good. Coming back to ourselves not only enriches our own lives but enriches the lives of those around us, creating a ripple effect that is far-reaching.

COUNT YOUR BLESSINGS

Why do you feel blessed today . . .?

....

....

....

....

....

....

....

....

....

....

....

....

....

....

....

....

....

....

3

Love of Life — the Adventurous Spirit

Your heart is in the ocean,
Your light is in the sun,
Your essence thrives on Mother Earth,
To stimulate our fun.

Much like love, adventure is ingrained in our wiring and produces a similar feeling of euphoria. It is through adventure that we discover our 'love of life', which makes us feel we are fully integrating with our environment and fulfilling our potential.

When you look at how adventure fires up your energy, you can see clearly that it excites and stimulates you, but sometimes there is an element of fear, too, as adventure often takes us into unknown territory. When we do extreme sports, for example, like skydiving, snowboarding or bungee jumping, scientists can now see that the amygdala — which is connected to the limbic system in the brain that governs emotions, sex drive, survival instincts and memory — becomes activated.

The amygdala's role is to recognise danger in unknown situations and therefore send the body into what is known as the 'fight or flight' mode. As your body prepares for impending danger, the brain releases hormones such as dopamine, adrenalin and endorphins to cope. These hormones are what stimulate our emotions and give us the 'high' or 'rush' connected with the states of happiness and euphoria.

Adrenalin's role is to prepare your body so that in those moments you are best primed to respond: you have a boost of energy and your senses (your sight and hearing, for example) become sharper. Dopamine prepares you to take risks and as a reward you experience emotions that make you feel good such as bliss, euphoria and motivation, while stimulating your sense of curiosity and excitement. Endorphins help ease any physical and mental pain you may experience and give you that sense of wellbeing, much like an opiate, to calm and soothe the senses.

So, when people seek the stimulation of adventure, whether it be a walking holiday in a country they've never visited before, signing up for a singles' holiday, learning a new language or doing anything that takes them out of their comfort zone, their brain is releasing hormones that allow them to fully engage with that activity and will assist them on that journey. Whenever we come across a new experience and embrace it, giving it our all, we embrace adventure.

When our brain is in the latter stages of development as teenagers, we are hardwired to pursue new experiences, take risks and experiment with sensations. This is what is known as the refining stage of our brain's wiring.

During that stage of a teenager's life, however, they don't have the self-control or common sense that adults with a fully-formed brain have, because the prefrontal cortex develops last, and this is the problem-solving, self-monitoring and decision-making part of the brain. It's understandable that, with hormones contributing to the mix, teenagers therefore tend to take impulsive risks. As risk-taking involves the possibility of success or failure, young people often need nurturing and guidance to take healthy risks, rather than those that will inhibit their wellbeing.

Life without adventure is like life without love. We can take this one stage further to understand why we need adventure. Studies have shown that people who love extreme sports go into what's called 'the zone', which psychologists say is when the mind is at its optimal state of consciousness or 'flow' and in its peak state of performance. This is much like how we feel when we're in a loving relationship and on a date, on holiday in a romantic setting or in any situation where we are totally focused on that person.

Many extreme sports can become addictive because of the very nature of how we respond to our rush of hormones, so it is recognised that people who retire from sports often suffer a kind of low or depression as their drug is no longer stimulated within them.

Adventure is not all about risk and extremes, but we're all programmed to desire it, as our ancestors once lived in a constant state of 'fight or flight' in order to survive. Satisfying our 'adventurous spirit' is our body's way of allowing ourselves the pleasure of fully interacting with the world when our lives have become stagnated and we have moved into the realms of routine or boredom. This is when we feel the need to create change and, above all, bring love into our lives. This kind of love does not rely on others, but it opens our curiosity and spirit, making us feel more alive and connected to our environment and the unknown.

Scientists have discovered that a part of our brain called the ventral striatum is fired up whenever we do something that takes us out of our comfort zone, and so it's known as the 'seat of adventure'. In our ancestors, this part of the brain would have been stimulated constantly, and so it is ingrained in us to find it satisfying. Zen masters liken this activation when we go into 'the zone' to a state of meditation, awareness or mindfulness. It's like a switch that takes us from what we believe to be our limitations into a state that creates possibility — and that's what keeps us coming back for more, as when we get hooked on a sport, for example.

When I was only nineteen my father died unexpectedly. Up until then I'd had my life pretty much mapped out for me to go to college and university to qualify as an interior designer and work in the family business.

When I lost my father, I lost all sense of who I was and what I was to become. I felt all alone in the world, with no real friends or family, and isolated myself from everyone in order to escape anything associated with my father. I ended up attracting a partner who was old enough to be my father (not surprisingly) and through him I discovered adventure. He was an avid skydiver and every moment spent with him was exciting. Inevitably, however, the relationship fizzled out after about eighteen months and I was back with my isolation, grief and uncertainty.

Desperate to feel again the high that the relationship had given me, I decided to take up skydiving myself in order to be around the exciting people we'd often hung out with who had made me feel so good. So I signed up for a parachute training course.

My ex had moved to Australia, and while it seemed exciting and petrifying going through the training, the satisfaction I felt when I used to spend time with him and the people he skydived with was not the same. I pushed myself to be there every moment that I was not working in order to try to feel the same feeling I once had. I started to become accepted by my fellow skydivers, although deep down I'm sure the people who were there knew I was only filling a void in my life.

Weekends were thrilling and exhilarating as we lived purely on adrenalin, and when we weren't throwing ourselves out of small aircraft, we were partying and having fun. However, when I drove home each Sunday, I had an awful feeling of longing in my stomach and an aching loneliness. During the week, I was low, depressed and longed for the weekends so that I could feel my high once more. This went on for about a year until finally I quit. Despite making friends with some of the other skydivers, they were not my people and, sadly, I felt it in my heart that I had to let go.

All the money I'd invested in training and equipment, the double shifts of working a full-time job during the day and then working in a local country club in the evenings in order to afford my extravagantly expensive hobby, finally burned me out. The more I tried to throw myself into work during the week in order to suppress my loneliness and the more I threw myself into making the most of every moment at the weekend with my new friends, the more I realised I was running away from myself.

Finally, I had to take stock of my life before I crashed. I knew the risks I was taking were more and more extreme, so the likelihood of me coming to some awful end was evident to the friends I hung out with. I recognised that I needed people in my life, but more than that, I needed adventure — in a form that was less about high risk and more about a balanced and grounded way of experiencing it.

Finally, I left that part of my life — and the people who had been quick fixes — behind and applied to work in ground operations at the airport. There I found people like myself who wanted adventure and to travel, but who sought a more balanced and safer way to experience it. During that time, I not only found my people, but discovered that I *loved to be* with people and had a natural empathy towards them. This was how I finally found what I wanted to do with my life: helping others.

Our authentic adventurous spirit will always reveal what we long to achieve when we invest in our self-love and therefore honour our truth.

The theta-beta swing

Many people suffer from what I refer to as the 'theta-beta' swing. This is when we seek temporary highs or a rush of euphoria that gives us a quick fix, a temporary distraction from everyday life as a way to avoid facing challenges or what really needs to be changed.

These 'distractions' could be overindulgence with food or alcohol, they may involve drug-taking or investing time in practices that are detrimental to our health and wellbeing, such as too much television, game-playing or even exercise. Whatever the distraction, it can become like a drug and increased time spent on those kinds of activities can only ever be a short-lived, temporary fix that has no long-term benefits.

The same could also be said for spiritual practices if they are used as a crutch. Some people in the early stages of their spiritual awareness find that euphoric sense of wellbeing from doing their practice, workshops or being in groups with other like-minded people, but when they go back to their everyday life, they find that they are once again facing difficulties and lower-level vibrations. Because they feel the euphoria of spiritual practice, they will keep returning to it while perhaps not learning the vital lessons and not doing the necessary work to make the changes needed to create a better everyday experience. These people may become what is referred to as 'spiritual junkies'.

This again is the theta-beta swing, which refers to the two frequencies that relate to these two opposing states of mind. Beta is the frequency of mind for logic and reason, and we go into this state when we're working things out in our head, when we're under pressure, in stressful situations or simply running for a bus or at the gym. It's the frequency that we go into for certain daily functions, but only for as long as is necessary to help us achieve our goals or overcome challenges. This frequency is not designed for extended periods of time, simply because we can suffer burnout. It's like only using one foot to pedal a bicycle. It's possible to do this over short periods, but over time your body will become incredibly fatigued from all the exertion of propelling yourself with one leg only. Taking a one-sided approach to practice is just as defeating as committing to no practice in the first place.

The theta frequency of mind, on the other hand, gives us the feeling of being whole and complete, and when experienced in excess can lead to one being too detached from life. Some people want to avoid life altogether by going into the 'zone' or 'flow' by indulging in certain activities that create that euphoria. If out of balance, however, there's a danger that they will rely on those activities to escape issues they don't want to face. This creates a swinging motion as the person is constantly trying to escape one way or the other.

When I first started to discover spirituality, this was exactly what I experienced, as I did every kind of practice I could to escape from the pain of my everyday world. The more I discovered ways to practice, the more time I spent immersed in them until I hardly felt I was here on this earth anymore. It was only when I discovered how to find balance through satisfying my innate need for adventure that I finally found a balanced way to create my 'zone' that was conducive to my health and wellbeing. This helped me to learn the necessary lessons to grow and to take the right action in order to find my 'happy place'.

We all have a happy place, and it can be reached by incorporating adventure into your life in the short-, mid- and long-term to create inner growth and fulfilment and to satisfy your innate desires. As a result, when you seek out relationships, you will attract the right ones, because you will be resonating on a frequency that fulfils your desires, and the people you connect with will in turn have fulfilled their own desires and their frequency will therefore match yours.

What tantalises your adventurous taste buds?

I've mentioned bungee jumping and skydiving as examples of extreme sports, and you may be the type of person who wants that kind of adventure. You may have always had a hankering to go white-water rafting, abseiling or caving. Just because you haven't had the time, money or opportunity, it doesn't mean that it can't happen. Your higher self has buried these desires deep in your subconscious so that when the opportunity does arise and you are operating at the right frequency, you will have the chance to experience them.

Our adventurous spirit is already mapped out in our personality blueprint, and everyone's desires, wishes and dreams are unique to them, but you can discover what they are when you 'feel' what your heart is telling you. And your angels of love can help reveal to you not only what they are, but how to achieve them. Here are some ideas that may tantalise your adventurous taste buds:

The Great Wall of China
If you have a hankering to walk the longest wall in the world and tread the path of an ancient defensive structure through rugged mountains and awe-inspiring scenery in northern China, then this wall — built over 2000 years ago, over different dynasties, to protect various borders — may well set your heart alight.

The wall itself spans over 13,000 miles; walkers can enjoy just a taste of the wall or a fuller, heartier experience — it's your journey, it's up to you. People often have the Great Wall of China on their bucket list, as something to experience at least once in their lifetime.

The Camino de Santiago

This is definitely one adventure that I've got on my bucket list, as I love walking and travel combined. Thousands of people walk this rite of passage every year and it is deemed a pilgrimage for those who love walking and engaging in a spiritual journey. Many people walk the whole route, which starts in Saint-Jean-Pied-de-Port near Biarritz in France and stretches 780 km (almost 500 miles) to the cathedral of Santiago de Compostela in north-west Spain.

The history of this pilgrimage dates back to the ninth century and it is said that Christian pilgrims discovered the remains of St James (the first disciple of Jesus) in Jerusalem and took them to bury him at the cathedral of Santiago de Compostela as he's the patron saint of Spain. The pilgrimage has been walked by millions since. The landscape en route includes ancient villages, towns and cities as well as vineyards and the French Pyrenees.

I was first inspired by this journey when I read Shirley MacLaine's book *The Camino: A Pilgrimage of Courage*. Many other authors have written about this extraordinary adventure, such as Paulo Coelho and Sonia Choquette, but it was reading Shirley's account that touched something in my heart, and it has remained there ever since.

They say that the Camino is not about getting from beginning to end, but the daily journeys, which are all adventures in their own right. Much like we should live our lives, each day gives the opportunity to find adventure.

The Great Barrier Reef

Some people are simply drawn to the ocean, some want the adventure of travelling to the other side of the world to explore unknown territories and some may have a particular love for our planet and a passion to help preserve it for generations to come.

The Great Barrier Reef is an enormous, sprawling, multi-coloured reef that spans over 135,000 square miles. It is known as the largest living structure on earth and has formed slowly over millions of years from tiny corals dying in vast numbers and forming hard skeletons of limestone. Amazingly, these structures only grow at a rate of around half an inch per year.

For ocean lovers, this is heaven, as here you can discover over 400 different species of coral, over 2000 different species of fish, 4000 species of mollusc and even 250 species of shrimp.

Divers love the warm waters and the diverse plant life, where sea turtles, dolphins and sharks can be observed. A World Heritage Site since the early 1980s, it is now protected, as this glorious spectacle attracts almost two million tourists a year.

The Orient Express

For those who seek the beauty and romance of the golden age of travel by rail, the Orient Express is for you. This luxury trip offers much more than fine dining and your own private compartment rich in 1920s décor; it's the chance to experience breathtaking scenery on your journey from the iconic cities of London and Paris, through the Swiss Alps, the Italian Dolomites and the Brenner Pass until you finally reach Venice, known as the 'floating city'.

From around the 1860s, trains were being modernised with the latest technology and luxury furnishings until finally the Venice Simplon-Orient-Express was born in the 1920s, marking the zenith of high-class travel across Europe. During the Second World War, however, borders were closed, marking the end of an era for this kind of travel, but then a wealthy rail enthusiast, James B. Sherwood, spent millions locating the vintage carriages and restoring them to their original splendour. To many, this is a once-in-a-lifetime adventure, and a chance to step back in time. It's a journey of romance, celebrating not only the history of the train, but also the love that was poured into rebirthing it.

Swimming with dolphins

Dolphins have an incredible ability to emit the alpha frequency, which resonates with our 'best self' and puts us in our 'happy place'. Studies have shown that when children and adults with learning difficulties, pain, depression or anxiety are exposed to dolphins, it improves their wellbeing.

Many people feel an affinity with these playful marine mammals, which may well come from the fact that science suggests we once evolved from the ocean ourselves some 540 million years ago. So perhaps our connection with the sea — which stimulates a sense of tranquillity, especially when we hear the sound of waves gently lapping the shore, like the sound of our own breath as we inhale and exhale — is a reminder of where we come from.

Although the thought of swimming with dolphins in captivity is not something that would appeal to many, there are opportunities around the world to experience them in their natural habitat. There are many species of dolphin that can be found around the Azores, Mexico, Central America, the Red Sea in Egypt, Fiji, Greece and Hawaii, to name but a few locations. And if you seek out responsible travel guides who have an empathy towards the freedom these incredible creatures deserve, then diving enthusiasts, ocean lovers and adventure-seekers alike can experience dolphins in all their glory, while retaining a mutual respect for our respective places on this planet.

The Grand Canyon

Studies are now revealing that the Colorado River started carving through the rock in Arizona and creating smaller canyons some 70 million years ago, to form the Grand Canyon that stands today.

The Colorado River itself is known for its magnificent canyons and white-water rapids and is a water source for 40 million people. You can visit one of the 11 National Parks along its pathway as well as the Grand Canyon itself, which is 277 miles long and 18 miles wide.

The expansiveness and breathtaking beauty of this vast landscape gives us a sense of freedom, yet reminds us of how beautiful our planet is and that we are but a minute part of it. Many find this a life-changing experience that reminds them how precious our world is and that we must respect its magnificence.

We were born to be creative and find adventure

Embracing our adventurous spirit is not just about setting lifetime goals, but also the mid- and short-term goals. Much like a river, our journey through life will take us through calm waters, winding routes of natural wonder and sometimes, as we hit challenges, rapids.

Adventure reminds us of our connection to this glorious planet and the amazing, expansive opportunities we have to enjoy its magnificence. Setting goals to bask in adventurous activities stimulates our love of life, no matter how great or small the experience.

To feed our soul and nurture our love of life, every day we should incorporate some kind of adventure, whether it be taking a new journey to work, making new friends or learning something that stimulates our thirst for knowledge. Coming out of our comfort zone or doing something creative satisfies our adventurous nature and reminds us that we are fully living this experience.

Despite how serious, complicated or painful their challenge is when they first visit me, I always encourage my clients to find what they love, as it's one of the most important aspects of their nature. Often it's deeply buried, ignored or even denied through a culmination of circumstances that have accrued over time.

Nonetheless, slowly but surely, with their angels of love, we unfold what fear and negative programming are shielding them from to discover their passion and love for life once more. This often reveals their creative or adventurous spirit.

Adelia contacted me as she was going through an incredibly difficult divorce, was experiencing challenges with her colleagues at work, had financial worries and felt alone, despite having moved to Australia from her homeland of Malaysia many years before.

Having come from a large and protective family, which had given her all the love and stability she had needed growing up, as she started her university years in a foreign land she experienced anxiety, detachment and isolation. Her family supported her through a challenging start to her university years which helped her to find her footing, yet several years into her career, she spiralled once again into depression through overwork.

Her routine of almost eighty hours a week at work had all but stifled the joy from her life and it was during that dark period that she met the man she would go on to marry and later divorce. Despite working hard at trying to move up the career ladder, she was challenged by colleagues and missed opportunities, and her marriage inevitably failed as there was a huge void in her life.

When I started working with Adelia, I introduced her to her angels of love by helping her to slow her pace of life down in order to find her 'song line', or rather, her unique vibration that works in harmony with the planet and all who reside on it. Through a series of sessions over a number of months, Adelia managed to move gradually through a tricky divorce. Where she had been blocked and controlled by her husband before, suddenly the Universe started to reveal to her that it had her back. Her angels of love were with her constantly and eventually she came through the separation from her husband, and the outcome benefited both of them. It surprised her that she was no longer resentful, and felt reassured that justice had played out for their greater good.

Adelia had by then created the space she needed to clearly see which other areas of her life no longer satisfied her and trusted her angels of love, listening to them in quiet meditation in order to find her joy once more. When I asked her what her creative passions were, at first she chose salsa dancing and pottery as her choices, but as her angels of love took her deeper within her meditations she discovered that, in fact, she wanted to take singing lessons, walk and travel.

She signed up for a local walking group in her area where she met like-minded people who opened her adventurous spirit even more. Surprised by her own courage, she booked to go to Tasmania on her own — something she would never have done before — and realised that there was a much bigger world out there, one that she could explore without limits.

Adelia found her adventurous spirit through her angels of love, who have helped her see far beyond the protective limitations she first put upon herself all those years ago when she shut down. Today, her life is governed by her love of adventure and she is now looking to incorporate travel into her work in the hope of achieving both personal fulfilment and success in her career.

Adelia's example shows that when we pay attention to our innate adventurous spirit and allow our angels of love to guide us, we can find our place in this world and fulfil our deepest desires.

Visualisation meditation to discover your adventurous spirit

Often people don't know what kind of adventure they want to experience, so using visualisation allows us to connect deep down with our angels of love to discover our unique creative expression. I often use this meditation to help clients discover theirs. You can record this meditation so that you can play it back later — and be mindful of reading it as slowly as you feel is right for you in order to benefit from it fully. This is great to repeat as often as you like, as visualisation is powerful, healing and helps us to manifest our desires. With the help of the natural law of attraction, sending this powerful message to the Universe through the guidance of your angels of love can be life-changing and magical.

Find yourself a quiet and comfortable place to sit where you won't be disturbed for a while. Turn off all phones and allow yourself some time to go within to connect with your angels of love. Make sure you are comfortable, with your back supported and your feet planted firmly on the ground, so that you feel supported by the earth.

Take a moment to check that your body is relaxed. Close your eyes and take a deep breath in. On the exhalation, imagine that you are breathing out any tension in your body so that it releases down through your feet, into the earth, and is transmuted into positive energy. Take another deep breath in and as you exhale, imagine that a pure white light is pouring down from the highest of the Divine, down through the top of your head, and imagine that this white light is filling your body from head to toe to purify, cleanse and energise you.

Breathe normally for a while as you sit with this feeling of relaxation, knowing that you're connecting with Source. Take as long as you need to feel that energising white light fill every part of your body. Now take another deep breath and imagine that white light is flowing out of your body to fill your aura – the energy field that surrounds you – and know that it is cleansing and healing your energetic body, your mind, emotions and spiritual self. Take as long as necessary to feel that the light has been fully absorbed into your aura.

When you feel ready, call upon your angels of love to guide you through a visualisation that will help you discover

*your adventurous spirit. 'Angels of love, help me discover my
adventurous spirit through your loving guidance, if it be for
the highest good of all!'*

*Now breathe normally and count downwards from 100 to
one, counting slowly for the recording. When you reach the
count of one, imagine that you are in a waiting room and are
facing a purple door. This is your magic door that, when
opened, will allow you to step into your first adventure. It's in
the land of plenty, a magical place where anything is possible.
Know that when you open that door, you will step into a place
that your heart is calling for you to discover – somewhere that
offers you limitless possibilities, excitement, joy and fulfilment.*

*Now, when you feel ready and knowing and trusting that
your angels of love are there to guide you through your
adventure, reach for the door handle and slowly open the
door and step out of the room into your land of plenty.*

*You may experience a place that you recognise, or it may
even be imaginary. It may be somewhere you've been before
and want to explore further, or it may even be an activity
that you wish to pursue. Whatever your adventure is, trust
that it will appear. Don't judge it, but as you see the image
form on the mental screen of your mind, let it sit with you
for a while. Allow your angels of love to guide you through
your adventure. Let them take you on a journey and fill your
senses with colour, as you take in what's in front of you,
around you and behind you as your door is no longer there.*

*You may have discovered that you're on a beach, near a
waterfall, in a park or on a mountain. You may be in a*

tranquil space basking at a retreat. You may be surrounded by a meadow or on a river cruise. Whatever your adventure, allow yourself to become fully immersed in the experience.

You are now trusting and allowing your experience to unfold with your angels of love, so allow the visual of your adventure to fully emerge in your mind and don't worry if it doesn't happen for you straight away; just be patient — wait until you see a scene start to take shape in front of you and allow that to expand. If you feel the image is disappearing or not as clear at any point, just breathe deeply and check your body to make sure you feel calm and relaxed.

Once you feel comfortable with what your angels of love are guiding you through visually, allow your senses to take in the sounds around you. Just allow them to filter into your mind and notice the different sounds. Now that sight and sound are expanding in your mind, allow your other senses to awaken. Notice any smells around you, perhaps from the scent of flowers or the earth beneath you. Reach out in your visualisation and see if you can touch anything, such as plants, trees or the grass beneath your feet. Finally, if food is part of your experience or perhaps water from a natural spring, allow your sense of taste to explore it.

Sit with this experience for a few moments longer while you bask in the magic of your adventure in the land of plenty.

Finally, when you feel ready to return, say. 'Thank you, angels of love, for showing me such a magical experience.

*Please show me how to allow my adventurous spirit to come
into my life when it is for the highest good of all. Thank you
and it is so!'*

*When you're ready to return to the place where you
began this journey, imagine that another purple door has
appeared in front of you. Walk up to the door, turn the
handle and walk through it, knowing that you will carry this
magical experience with you and that your angels of love
will guide you to unlock your adventurous spirit in the
physical world.*

*Now, once you're back in the room, shut the door behind
you, slowly count from one to five and then open your eyes
when you're ready.*

You should now feel relaxed, energised and at peace, but
above all you should feel secure in the knowledge that your
angels of love will guide you towards your unique adventurous spirit when the time is right.

Your light bulb moment

Now that you've experienced the visualisation meditation
for your adventurous spirit, you will have opened your heart
energy centre to connect with all of your consciousness.
As you connect through that energy centre, inspiration,
possibilities and opportunities merge together, all waiting
for you to embrace the moment.

Take a moment to write in your journal, on a piece of paper or somewhere that is meaningful for you. You may even want to record this on your computer so that you can print it off and see it each and every day as an affirmation of what you wish to create for your adventurous spirit.

Take a few deep breaths and feel yourself connecting with your angels of love. Now ask them to show you a bucket list of adventures that you and your loved ones would love to experience in your lifetime. These can be short-, mid- and long-term goals, so allow all ideas to flow and write them down without judgement as they come to you.

Do not analyse them or try to work out how you'll achieve these things; just write them down and continue until you feel you've created your list. If you want to add to this list at any time later, when you feel inspiration manifest itself in some way, then you can always do so. The point of this exercise is to open the door and trust that when the time is right, and if it's for the highest good of all, your adventurous desires will appear to you in the form of opportunities and synchronistic messages, which will help you to achieve your goals.

Now place this bucket list somewhere where you can refer to it either daily or every so often, to remind yourself that you have the ability to allow your adventurous spirit to shine.

Chapter summary

Embracing our adventurous spirit enables us to open our heart and fully express our love of life. We all have an innate explorer within us and each of us is aware at a subconscious level what our journey entails, what lands we want to explore and what discoveries we wish to make. Our angels of love can guide us through our own personal navigation system, which carries our vessel safely through unknown waters, and help us to embrace all aspects of the adventure that will follow. They include excitement, wonder, joy, even fear and uncertainty, but these feelings will allow us to grow spiritually, expand our awareness and find courage to go on to even greater adventures.

COUNT YOUR BLESSINGS

Why do you feel blessed today . . . ?

....
....
....
....
....
....
....
....
....
....
....
....
....
....
....
....
....
....

4

Relationships

Loved ones, friends and family,
Our neighbours, old and new,
Each one of us shines a unique truth
To give a different view.

The most profound experiences we can have in life are our relationships with others: partners, family members, friends, associates, neighbours and people we come across in day-to-day life. Whether long-term, temporary or fleeting, these relationships are developed based on our own individual needs.

When we work on loving ourselves and finding our love of life, we start to become aware of how our love for our environment is a direct reflection of how we interact with others in this world. The more aware of this we become, the more we can improve our connectedness with others.

Our environments

Creating a space for love in our homes encourages our angels to help us match this in our lives in a healthy, harmonious way. Feng shui is a Chinese belief that governs spatial awareness and orientation in our homes and businesses. It relates to 'chi', or the flow of energy, and encourages us to look at the design and layout of buildings so that they have a favourable effect on the lives of those living and working in them.

My angels of love first introduced me to feng shui when I was going through difficulties with my marriage. I invited a feng shui practitioner to my home and was amazed at how they picked up on the issues I had in my relationships with myself and my husband. I started to make immediate changes to my home and over time could see the evident transformation in my life as my home finally became a place that reflected my mindset.

Your bedroom

Your bedroom represents your relationship with yourself and your partner. If your room is cluttered and untidy, this will be reflected in both of these relationships. By decluttering and creating order in your personal and intimate space, you can create a feeling of wellbeing for yourself and allow positive energy to flow into your relationship, which will help you to overcome challenges.

Your bed

The position of your bed can often have an adverse effect on relationships or block you from attracting love into your life. If you have your bed pushed against the wall, then whoever sleeps on the side that is up against the wall will experience a feeling of being trapped in the relationship. This can also block potential relationships from forming.

Ideally, the bed should be equidistant from the walls on either side to give both partners equality in the relationship. Also, the bed would ideally be on the opposite side of the room to the door, although not directly in front of it or this will have people coming into your intimate space far too quickly. Being able to see the door from your bed, however, enables you to welcome your loved one into your space, so place a mirror opposite the door if possible.

Clear space for a relationship

If you are single and want to attract a partner into your life, look at your bedroom to see where you need to create space to allow that relationship to be invited in. Having overstuffed wardrobes and a bed full of cuddly toys does not send the right message, so clear wardrobes and drawers, perhaps invest in new bedding and make your room feel welcoming to the partner you envisage sharing that space with you. At night, before you go to sleep and with your eyes closed, ask your angels of love to help you connect with your loved one and encourage them to come into your life.

Remove past relationship reminders

It's natural for us to keep letters, photos or gifts from past relationships from a sense of nostalgia. But if we wish to encourage new relationships or mend a broken one, it's vital to look through your home for anything that 'attaches' you to the energy of old relationships that ended badly or caused negativity in your life. This is especially important if these objects are kept in the bedroom. Remove them with a blessing; it will help you let go of the past and any negative energy that is holding you back and allow space for healthy, loving relationships to flourish.

Lucky symbols to attract love

In China, Japan and South Korea, mandarin ducks, also known as 'love ducks', are a symbol of love and marriage. Bought as ornaments, they are traditionally kept in the home to enhance and attract love. According to the principles of feng shui, placing these ducks on the south-west side of your bedroom brings luck and positive energy to your love life and encourages a beautiful marriage. Adding symbols of love to your bedroom, such as hearts, rose quartz crystals, pink candles or pictures of couples in loving settings, sends a powerful message to the Universe to affirm what you desire.

Create a tranquil space

Our bedroom should be a place of peace and tranquillity, so remove any exercise machines or equipment that represent physical activities, as this energy will otherwise be absorbed into your relationship and create a sense of effort within it, as opposed to natural flow.

Be open to love

Doors are often seen as symbolic of allowing people into your life, so it's important that the main entrance to your home is welcoming. Doors that are difficult to open or creak can have an adverse effect on how we invite people into our life. Likewise, our bedroom door should be easy to open fully in order to welcome a loving relationship into our life. The hallway, too, is the entranceway into our life. Make sure it is clutter-free so that energy can flow freely and people don't have 'obstacles' to overcome in order to reach you.

Create a vision board for your ideal loving relationship

Collect images that represent your ideal relationship, including what type of home you would live in and what sort of holidays and activities you would enjoy together. Incorporate symbolic pictures that build an image of the type of life you'd love to share together. If you are single and looking for love, this will enable you to send a visual representation to your angels of love for them to fulfil your desires. If you want to improve an existing relationship, you can ask your partner to share this task with you so you can find a mutual vision of your enhanced future together.

Place the board somewhere you will notice it every day so that your angels of love will feel your heart connecting to it; they can then help to create your wishes through the law of attraction.

Janice, a client of mine, first came to me some years ago, as she was a chronic hoarder, in debt and had a narcissistic husband who constantly controlled her. She was retired and she felt her life was empty; with no friendships and no social activities in her life, she was depressed and alone. I discovered that, when she was younger, she'd been abused by those who were in positions of authority and this had led to a life filled with more abuse and torment throughout much of her married life. She had been unhappy and often manipulated, and felt powerless.

I first started working with her when she came to one of my workshops and it was evident there was absolutely no self-love in her life, but I introduced her to her angels of love so that she could ask for guidance in making the necessary changes to find peace, love and contentment.

Slowly but surely, she incorporated practices of self-love, she joined groups where she met like-minded new friends and started to create a social life that supported her desires. She booked on to courses for empowerment, which helped her become more assertive, and over time she started to confront her fears. She spoke up for herself more often and stood up not only to the husband who was controlling her, but also the abusers from her past.

Amazingly, she not only sought prosecution for the crimes committed against her, which resulted in justice being served, she was also awarded hefty compensation for the persecution she'd suffered as a child.

Janice felt confident that she could get on with life now that so much change had occurred. I didn't hear from her for a year, but out of the blue she got in touch, feeling very distressed. She still had her friendships and social activities and even attended some courses whenever possible, but she'd stopped her practices of self-love.

Her hoarding had never been tackled, so she was still living in a home crammed with belongings, which over-whelmed her. She had also lost all her compensation money and was back in serious debt. She felt even more desperate than before because she felt financially tied to her husband and powerless about her hoarding and had nowhere left to turn.

I gently reminded Janice that by calling on her angels of love and reintroducing self-love, she would be able to get herself back on track. We worked together over the next few months, receiving guidance from her angels, and gradually she started to see great changes. She found the strength to work with a debt charity, who set up a monthly budget for her, and created a 'wish box' for her angels of love, so that whenever there was something she desired, she would put a picture of it in her box so that they could help her receive it.

One of her habitual negative habits was to procrastinate and spend time doing the little things in her house that didn't need doing in order to avoid the things she really ought to be doing for herself. So she created a calendar that held her accountable every day to recording activities of self-love. As her mindset had slipped back into thoughts of unworthiness, Janice started to record how she was valuing herself every day with activities that gave her self-love instead, and eventually she reached financial stability, cleared her cluttered home (which had been a reflection of her 'cluttered mind') and spent more time with loving people and immersed in loving situations.

Through small but meaningful changes to her attitude, she created a whole new scenario in her daily life. Instead of spending her whole day worrying, procrastinating and doing small jobs that never seemed to end in an effort to avoid the things she dreaded tackling, her day could be filled with going to a group meeting, having coffee and a catch-up with friends, seeing her physio for her health and wellbeing, and spending two hours clearing out her house, separating the clutter into things she no longer wanted and no one else would, things for the charity shop and things she wanted to keep.

Eventually, Janice managed to clear two-thirds of her house over a period of months and finally found the freedom she had craved for years to move away from her husband and start a new life. Creating a clear, tranquil space, free from toxicity, helped to match the intentions of her mind, enabling her to attract what she wanted into her life.

As Janice continued to detoxify her home, her power increased, her voice grew stronger and her life changed, finally bringing her the peace, love, adventure and meaningful relationships that she deserved.

The law of attraction in relationships

As we are first and foremost composed of energy and are governed by the law attraction (i.e. we attract that which our mindset is focused on, consciously or unconsciously), our energy state is often reflected back onto our relationships. When we look at the relationships that are playing out around us and see them as happy, we can often judge ourselves or our partner harshly for our own failings, but this creates a false sense of reality. All relationships face challenges, but happy, harmonious couples simply work together with a higher level of awareness in order to overcome challenges.

So, when we find we attract negative behaviours in ourselves or others because of our past experiences, it's an opportunity for us to look at what is going on inside, to learn and often to heal the negative programming that may have caused the challenge. Every connection we make with another person is unique and therefore going within will reveal the solutions we need to be aware of and the lessons we need to learn in order to release ourselves and the other person from that which locks us in disharmony.

Whether it be in a long-term, loving relationship or a fleeting moment between passers-by, we each communicate subconsciously through our energy field, which acts as a mirror to both participants. In these moments, everything seems to be going on at once: first, we communicate through our logical mind and physical self, by listening and speaking; we pick up subtleties through body language; then we communicate through our thoughts and feelings, and pick up messages through smell and the subconscious. Not only that, we are reflecting back to the other person an insight into how they are feeling about themselves.

When we're in alignment with our true nature (i.e. we practise self-love and love of life), then we have the power to deal proactively with anything we may see reflected back at ourselves. However, if we are in a state of imbalance and powerlessness and therefore not protected, we will find ourselves reacting to what we don't like to see in ourselves, and this creates conflict. Likewise, when two people don't like what they see in each other's mirrors, their conflict can spiral out of control, as neither can recognise how to get out of the cycle of deprivation.

Often conflict arises between people that relates to how our memory bank loops back to the past in search of a similar situation; we look at the end result last time in order to try to help ourselves in the present. More often than not the current situation is a whole new experience and your intention is to create a positive result, yet still your conditioning is dictating your response based on your past. This is known as the 'loop effect', which people who keep attracting the same types of dysfunctional relationships or situations sometimes experience.

A client of mine named Steven came to see me when his third long-term relationship ended in a very similar way to the previous two. Each relationship had lasted a couple of years and, in all three cases, they made plans for a long-term future together as they were happy, had much in common and spent as much time together as they possibly could.

When Steven came to me, we asked for his angels of love to help. His angels of love showed me that there was a pattern of coincidence with all three relationships. Each woman had had difficulties with her ex-partner and was in conflict with them even throughout their relationship with Steven. Steven did his utmost to give them confidence; he would give his all to them once they were over their conflict and detached from those energy-draining relationships and was instrumental in helping them find their power and voice through self-love.

Again coincidentally, as each woman found her power and voice, she abruptly ended her relationship with Steven, which broke his heart. They all moved out of his life suddenly, so he had no closure.

With the help of Steven's angels of love, we looked into his first significant long-term relationship and he shared that his girlfriend had left him out of the blue when he had chosen to go back into further study. She had explained that she could not bear him spending long hours studying and saw this as Steven giving more to his career than his relationship. This, she felt, was too much for her and she walked away. Steven was thrown into chaos and missed the opportunity to do what he wanted with his career and so never got on the first rung of the property ladder. This left him stuck in a job that could cover his rent, but would never enable him to progress and earn the potential he felt he deserved, or to buy a home.

Steven's angels of love also showed him that, because of the three break-ups that broke his heart, he felt that every long-term relationship he got involved in would end in heartache, be costly and would lead to him never getting the promotion or recognition he deserved in his career.

His angels of love encouraged him to take a radical leap of faith and, rather than live his life of safety and low-level risk, to start taking small steps out of his comfort zone to show him that self-love was safe and rewarding. Finally Steven broke his patterns of self-sabotage to find the love and life path he truly deserved. At last he had been able to see what had caused this pattern and had managed to break himself free of the negative conditioning that was holding him back, changing many aspects of his life that had failed him before in the process.

Knowledge and understanding of what patterns repeat themselves in your relationships allow you to reclaim your power,
enabling you to make the right choices and bring about the
necessary changes so that you can attract the relationships
that will serve your highest good. Just because we experience
negativity in relationships does not mean we have to keep
enduring it or that we will encounter further difficulties in
other relationships. It simply means that our angels of love
are trying to get our attention, to help us realise why we
attracted that negativity in the first place, so that we can
move on from struggle to a place of love.

When you discover recurrent patterns that play out nega-
tively in your life and you want to change them, you can ask
your angels of love to help you at night before you sleep.
The following steps will help you play your part in bringing
about this change, and the prayer that follows them can be
used to ask your angels of love for their help, too:

1. **Recognition and taking ownership.** This is not to say you
   should take full responsibility for what is happening on
   your side of the relationship, but it helps to take ownership
   of what is coming from you and causing a reaction in the
   other person because of their own issues. Relationships
   are a constant juggling act between negative and positive
   programming, which plays out in *all* experiences.

2. **Removing judgement** and incorporating acceptance allows you to neutralise the experience so that you can give a proactive response, as opposed to a reactive one. Often two people think they are both right (and perhaps they are), as they can only see the matter from their own perspective, based on their own experiences. Moving away from judgement eases the situation and helps you find a resolution.

3. **See the lesson,** as there is always something to learn. Your angels of love will help you see what you need to learn in order to heal the situation and, most importantly, move on so that the pattern is not repeated and you no longer have to go through that particular drama.

4. **Extend forgiveness** to yourself and the other person for their reaction or behaviour, as you are both trying to do your best, despite the negative programming. This releases you both from one another's programmes so that you can start from a level playing field.

5. **Be open and willing to change.** It's important to realise that change means being brave, overcoming fears and coming out of your comfort zone in order to grow and heal. In the long run you will become a better person for it, and you will have given the other person the opportunity to do so, too.

Night meditation to resolve relationship issues

Last thing at night before you sleep, sitting up in bed, with your eyes closed and the lights off, take a few deep breaths until you feel calm, tranquil and relaxed. Then say this small prayer:

Angels of love, I call upon you to hear my prayers to help bring about a resolution to my relationship difficulties with — — [say the name of the person]. Please help our relationship to heal so that we can find peace and have a greater understanding and compassion for one another and communicate from our higher selves for the greatest good of all. Help me recognise and learn the lesson I am being shown in this situation. Help me to remove judgement. I forgive myself and — — [say the name of the person] for any part we have played in this role that was not conducive to our wellbeing. I am open and willing to change, so please help me, angels of love, to recognise what I need to do to honour all relationships now and in the future.

Amen

Now picture yourself and the person involved in a setting where you are able to talk. The aim is to see your best selves communicating in harmony, peacefully and perhaps in a state of joy and love. Whatever the relationship is, see yourselves in your best light. You could be sitting together at the kitchen table over a coffee, in a restaurant over dinner, in the park walking together — whatever feels right for you.

Make sure you create a setting that represents the message you wish to send to your angels of love to show them your ideal outcome. The environment you are in is simply to give the right ambience for your angels of love.

Now see yourselves talking as if you're really engaging with one another, understanding one another and feeling at peace. See yourselves both speaking honestly and from the heart. If the other person is a partner, loved one or family member, you can send them love and see yourselves hugging. Whatever the relationship, see yourselves communicating with the outcome you desire so that you feel you have found a deeper connection from your higher selves.

Once you feel ready, trust that your angels of love have recognised your wishes and go to sleep.

For the next seventy-two hours, watch for signs from your angels of love of any action you might need to take to bring about change. Recognise any prompts or feelings that suggest what you can do to find the resolution you desire and record what changes come about within the relationship as a result – this will show your prayers have been answered. Often, just the prayer and visualisation will bring about change, so be open and ready to do what you feel is right, and be aware of what your angels of love are trying to communicate to you.

Putting the effort into understanding why relationships go through difficulty, why you seem to be blocked from attracting healthy relationships or seem always to repeat the same patterns allows you to have a more harmonious relationship with everyone, not just those you are in conflict with.

The power of positive relationships to effect the greater good far outweighs that of negative relationships. If you look at how families pass on negative conditioning to the younger generations, it's not surprising that we live in a world where so much war and conflict occurs. When we take a stand and take ownership of our thoughts and feelings towards others, we not only stop cycles of deprivation spreading to others, we in fact start to reverse the conditioning and influence in a positive, loving and harmonious way. Ultimately, this is why we're now seeing such a huge surge in awareness, mindfulness and spiritual practice, and a deeper faith that there is a greater force at play, helping us to make this a better world to live in.

Asking your angels of love how you can do your bit, however small, to make this a more loving and harmonious world will have an impact on the bigger picture. Once you become mindful of the consequences of your thoughts and feelings, you will have far greater influence on humankind and our planet than you can possibly imagine. Angels of love will always show their gratitude towards loving and giving people, so the more love you send out there into the world, the more you, your loved ones and the whole of humanity will benefit.

Your light bulb moment

Do you have doubt about a relationship that you're currently in or not had closure to a previous relationship because you worry that you ended it for the wrong reasons? This exercise will help you with decision-making if you're teetering on the edge in a relationship or want to know that you've moved on for good reason.

Find a quiet moment in your day and in your journal draw three columns, each with their own heading based on the points below, then ask your angels of love to help you to complete this exercise with openness and honesty. Write down in your three columns:

Your partner's good points — such as: thoughtful, generous, makes me laugh, loving, attractive, spontaneous, romantic, etc.

Things that irritate you about your partner but that you can accept with grace — such as: has a tendency to leave dirty dishes around the house, often leaves the loo seat up, never leaves their mobile phone alone . . . even when we're watching a film together, etc.

Things that you do not like or cannot accept — such as: has a tendency to lie, as they've been found out on numerous occasions; they're secretive, which makes me feel insecure; they've betrayed me with another partner, etc.

Now ask your angels of love to help you look at how compatible your current partner is, or your previous partner was, with you.

For a healthy and positive long-term relationship, you should have a long list in the first column, a few comments in the second and none in the third. If you have more comments in the second column, fewer in the first and none in the third, then you need to ask your angels to help you with self-love and to practise non-judgement and acceptance in order to see if this relationship is really for the long-term. Finally, if you have comments in all three columns then you really do need to look at whether this relationship is for you. Despite seeing the good points in your partner and being able to tolerate some of their irritating habits, if you have anything you cannot accept about them, you will not get over this or be able to come from a place of trust, openness, respect and, above all, love. This can be likened to a box of assorted chocolates. You know they are delicious and they're packaged well, but if you open the box and discover that they've gone off, no matter how much you want to eat them, you know they will make you sick if you try.

Sometimes letting go is hard, as we worry we'll be on our own, not invited to social events, blamed for a break-up or judged. We may feel guilt, insecurity, fear or anxiety, or just not want to end a relationship because of the other people involved. Realising the truth about a relationship, however, helps you take back your power, while asking your angels of love to help you heal and find resolution will support all those involved for the highest good. Even when relationships end, there are always new and positive beginnings.

Chapter summary

Relationships give us feedback about what we're processing internally in our subconscious mind. Whatever plays out in our relationship with others is a direct reflection of how we feel about ourselves and what kind of programmes we're running. By taking responsibility for whatever is playing out through this kind of dynamic, we can make necessary changes to our thoughts and beliefs in order to improve our relationships, remove ourselves from destructive cycles of behaviour and attract more loving and harmonious situations and people, who serve our highest good and that of all concerned.

COUNT YOUR BLESSINGS

Why do you feel blessed today . . .?

....

....

....

....

....

....

....

....

....

....

....

....

....

....

....

....

....

5

The Many Facets of Love

The many aspects time has shown,
Revealing what I know,
Have only made me realise
That I have so far to go.

'Emotion' in the *Oxford English Dictionary* is defined as '*a strong feeling deriving from one's circumstances, mood or relationships with others*'. Science, meanwhile, describes emotion as something that has evolved within us as a prompt to create automatic responses for survival.

Emotions manifest themselves as non-verbal expressions — such as feeling happy, hateful, loving, fearful, guilty, jealous, surprised or angry — and can be articulated through our body language.

Through various communication methods — conscious and unconscious, verbal and non-verbal — we can read what is going on with people, but it is through the non-verbal (i.e. through sensing the emotions within others and recognising how that has a knock-on effect within ourselves) that we can truly tell our heart or our higher self what is going on at any given moment.

Sometimes we cannot work out why we keep getting that 'feeling' that something is not right when we're with someone, or that we feel awkward, unsure or unsafe around someone. Likewise, we may be unable to explain why we feel surges of excitement, happiness, joy or contentment around people we barely know. This is all connected to our subconscious. Our emotions are our inner communication system alerting us to the truth about a situation, and, when we pay attention, they can reveal so much and help us make decisions.

Becoming mindful of our emotions helps to improve our mindset, self-worth and relationships. Dr Bach, for example, was a great bacteriologist, physician and pathologist who discovered thirty-eight different flower remedies during the 1920s and 1930s that were created from plant extracts and associated with human emotions. He defined a spectrum of human emotions ranging from joy at the top to boredom in the middle and then guilt, which was deemed the lowest human emotion.

Having suffered from depression himself, Bach was drawn to nature as it made him feel better. He then discovered that certain plants had the ability to transmute human emotions from negative to positive. His discovery led him to see that nature's blueprint, which is pure unconditional love, has a positive impact on our own when it comes into contact with our energy field. This is why it makes us feel so much better when we walk in the forest or sit in a tranquil garden, look out at the ocean or walk beside a natural river. Nature is designed to stimulate our higher self and promote health and wellbeing.

Dr Bach's remedies help transmute different negative emotions by uploading the higher emotions that are their opposite. This is much like how nature works – in harmony with itself. When there is a forest fire, for example, despite the fact that it causes devastation and loss of the natural surroundings, nature does not judge it to be wrong; it simply has a way of reconstituting itself in a positive way, replacing the scorched earth with enriched mineral soil so that new life can begin again.

This is how we learn as humans. When we see a negative situation change into something positive, it helps us to see that we have the ability to transform our own difficulties and limitations. Nature shows us that there is always a positive to every negative, and this helps us to see that there are many facets to our emotions and that they are simply a response to a given situation, aimed at encouraging us to do something about it.

Dr Bach recognised that sometimes we get stuck in our lower-level vibrations, as he did with depression, but that by using the power of nature, we can identify the lessons we need to learn (and in his case create a legacy to help others overcome negative emotions) and also restore ourselves to our higher self.

During the early stages of my work with clients, I was fascinated with how our bodies respond to people and situations, and how they reveal clues as to what is going on for us. I was naturally drawn to studying the power of the mind, healing, metaphysics and body language. I came across a couple of teachers who I worked with for over a year, studying physiology and anatomy, meditation, reflexology (so I could understand how the blueprint of our body is mapped out on our hands, feet and cranium), and it was then that I was first introduced to the Bach Flower Remedies.

At first, I couldn't possibly see how these tiny bottles of nature's essence could have such an impact on human beings. However, I started to introduce them to my clients as an addition to their transformation process and was amazed at how powerful they were. I could see that while I worked with the client to bring their negative programmes to the surface, our overall success was down to their determination to allow these emotions to be released. The flower remedies came into my life coincidentally when I asked my angels of love to help me help my clients with this missing link to their process.

I've never looked back and still use these remedies today, as they encourage my clients to be proactive and reveal their negative conditioning, as opposed to simply reacting, which just perpetuates and feeds the negative programmes all the more. Nature is unconditionally loving and will bring out our best self, and trusting that there is a positive to every negative helps to abate the oversensitive and dramatic feelings that work against us. We can then finally welcome in the new emotions that feed our higher self and replace the negative programmes in our blueprint with positive ones.

The positive facets of love

When we look at the many different stages of a loving relationship, it can involve a whole spectrum of emotions, reactions and situations. Greeting the many facets of love with acceptance, trust and understanding allows our higher self to embrace the journey with an authentic approach and an open heart, and to fully engage in each stage, allowing it to grow at its own pace for the highest good of both involved.

Each stage of love:
1. Fascination, interest, intrigue, attentiveness — as we're drawn to that person.

2. Pleasure, amusement, enjoyment, distraction, playfulness, relaxation — as we start to open up and form a connection.

3. Joy, bliss, ecstasy, thrill, euphoria, bonding, exclusiveness — as that love starts to seep into all aspects of our life.

4. Hope, desire, wishes, dreams, aspirations, longing, planning — as the relationship starts to develop into a possible long-term commitment.

5. Tranquillity, peace, calm, safety, certainty, contentment, togetherness — as trust builds.

6. Appreciation, respect, trust, gratitude, recognition, acceptance — as the relationship develops a deeper love and an acknowledgement of each other's differences emerges.

7. Fulfilment, satisfaction, pride, reward — as the relationship matures, both are encouraged to grow together yet the individual magic thrives.

8. Encouragement, inspiration, motivation, support, upliftment — the love that comes from becoming a better person because of each other.

9. Reverence, value, admiration, honour — when that love has matured enough to have withstood many of life's challenges and adventures.

Suzanna was a client of mine who came to me as she was tired of attracting unhealthy relationships. She was particularly drawn to those who were controlling and disconnected emotionally, and also had other challenges in her life, relating to lack of self-worth, depression and money troubles.

In the first session, I learned that her family had rejected her as a teenager and banished her from seeing them because she didn't comply with their religious beliefs, and so she was tossed out into the world with no guidance or security. She felt abandoned, lost, alone and fearful. Desperate to survive, this young girl attracted negative relationships and addictions, which soon spiralled out of control until finally she reached out for help.

I introduced Suzanna to her angels of love, we started a process of self-love and together intuited what flower remedies would help support her through her transformation. As Suzanna was on a high dose of antidepressants, it was important that she took time to allow her programmes to release in her own time, supported by the flower remedies, so that she was proactive in the process, rather than reactive.

She was open, trusting and above all dedicated to making the necessary changes that eventually helped release her from her depression and lessened her dependency on medication, which had controlled her in the past.

Suzanna went on to become a well-recognised person in her field, as she presented her own radio show, produced a newsletter and supported others through their own mental health issues. Today, she's in a committed, long-term relationship and has joy in her life, which is proving both fulfilling and productive. Her life is now reflecting how valued she is and what a rewarding member of her community she is now that she's found her 'family'.

Heartbreak and recovery

It's inevitable that heartbreak will come to us in our lifetimes, but it's how we deal with it that shapes how we move on. When we experience the different facets of love and the many phases we go through on that road to discovering who we are within a relationship, who our partner is and how we respond to that person, we can also be faced with the many ways in which love can create lower emotions.

Confrontation comes up when there's a miscommunication, when we don't like how the other person is behaving or when we just experience conflict within ourselves. Sometimes, the relationship is just meant to be for a short while in order for us to learn lessons about ourselves and others, and inevitably, if we care deeply for that person, that can create heartbreak, especially when we have invested so much time and energy into the relationship or thought it was for the long term.

A period of heartbreak is a time for us to heal. The pain can last for however long it takes to heal from that relationship, but we're designed to come out of it stronger and wiser, if we are able to embrace the experience, rather than hiding away or blocking it. If we push the heartache aside, it will come up again further down the line to demand healing and prompt lesson learning. Accepting heartbreak with love and grace towards yourself — and towards your partner if you can — will release you both from any karmic ties that could later hold you locked together or in cycles of repeated patterns.

Affirmations to release ourselves from any karma and to embrace all facets of love

You can copy out these affirmations and say them to your angels of love every day first thing in the morning as you wake and last thing at night before you sleep, in order to release yourself from any karma or negative conditioning that is stopping you from experiencing the full spectrum of love.

Your angels of love will respond to your request, but it is up to you to take the right action when they convey what they want you to be aware of or do. Be mindful of what signs and prompts you receive, encouraging you to take opportunities and recognise what needs to change in order to be fully aligned with your higher self.

The more you say these affirmations, the better the result will be, so try to say them as often as your heart tells you. Remember, if you say them once a day you will get good results, but if it's twice a day, you will get better results. Most importantly, saying them at the optimum times (first thing in the morning and last thing at night, when you are relaxed and therefore best able to communicate with your angels of love) will ensure that your messages are understood loud and clear.

Angels of love,
My heart energy centre is open fully and I allow all of life to flow through me to discern what is for my highest good.

*I am ready, able and willing to learn from all
relationships in order to grow and become my best self.*

*I embrace my higher self and project that out to all I meet
in order to attract back that which serves my highest good.*

*I am compassionate, loving and true to my higher self
and release all pain and heartache from any previous
relationships in order to experience every facet of love.*

My relationships are authentic and rewarding.

*I constantly strive to accept others for all that they are
and embrace their limitations with grace.*

*My capacity to love is limitless and I'm constantly
surrounded by loving people and loving situations.*

*Thank you, angels of love, for always guiding and
protecting me. I am grateful as always for your
unconditional love.*

Your light bulb moment

Bach Flower Remedies are now available around the world, although there are other essences available from many countries, such as the Australian Bush Flower Essences. I still recommend the Bach Flower Remedies to my Australian clients, but see what you feel drawn to, as you should trust your heart.

You can use flower remedies to help you through any time of challenge or when you're not attracting relationships for whatever reason. The best way to choose what flower remedies you need is to ask your angels of love to help you decide. I suggest you choose three flower remedies, which is what I choose for all my clients.

Get yourself a dowser or a pendant or even a wedding band or something hanging from a piece of cord — anything that will spin naturally and is weighted. Find a list of all the flower remedies in the range and write them out on a large piece of paper, or two if necessary, giving yourself enough room so that when you dowse over each name, the dowser doesn't cross over onto another name and confuse your reading.

Before you use the dowser over the names, hold it above your free hand. Set the dowser in motion slightly, until you feel it picking up energy and moving of its own accord, then ask your angels of love to show you a 'yes'. Once you see the dowser moving in a certain direction (clockwise, anti-clockwise or up and down), your angels of love are showing you that this will be the response 'yes'.

Stop the dowser from moving and repeat the process to find out from your angels of love which way it will move for a 'no' answer.

Once you have your yes and no responses, ask your angels of love to help you choose which flower remedies will help release you from any negative conditioning that is holding you back from having a happy and loving relationship. Going over each remedy on your list individually and being careful to reset your dowser each time, make a note of which ones respond to yes and which ones to no.

This may take practice, so you may want to first ask simple questions that you know have a yes or no answer to test your dowser over your hand. Once you feel confident, try it with the flower remedies until you find the ones you feel you are strongly being guided to take.

You can now check which emotions are out of balance by seeing which remedies you've chosen. Sometimes you will know why you've chosen them and sometimes it will come as a surprise. Trust that your angels of love know best and are guiding you, and order your chosen remedies so that you can take them as soon as you are ready to make a start with your process.

With your Bach Flower Remedies, take two drops of each and place them all together in a small bottle or glass of water and drink every day for thirty days.

Make notes in your journal at the beginning of what you want to achieve, and throughout the thirty days of what synchronicities you recognise. Then, at the end, note down what results or changes have occurred.

Remember, flower remedies are nature's way of amplifying your higher self and asking your angels of love to help you make the changes necessary for your highest good.

Chapter summary

Love can be experienced on many levels and recognising that love has so many facets allows us to embrace it, rather than judge it or hide from it when we feel we have failed or it isn't what we hoped it would be. Love is a whole language in itself, speaking to us through our emotions so that we can choose how we deal with it, and the results play out according to whether we're out of alignment with our authentic self or in alignment with our true nature. By accepting that we will always feel our truth, we honour our higher nature, and being open to all that life has to offer enables us to experience the whole spectrum of our emotions so that we can live life fully, rather than teeter on the brink of possibility.

COUNT YOUR BLESSINGS

Why do you feel blessed today...?

....

....

....

....

....

....

....

....

....

....

....

....

....

....

....

....

6

Unconditional Love

This gift you gave, a love so true,
Selfless, pure and bold,
Has shown me how to give my all
Until I'm wise and old.

Once upon a time, unconditional love was far more prevalent than it is today, because there was far less expectation from our partners. Loving someone unconditionally is the highest way of giving love, as you are loving with no judgement and no expectation of receiving anything in return. It can be recognised, perhaps, in the relationship between parents and children; despite how much they test your love, you would still give them your left kidney if they were sick.

Loving others unconditionally comes from loving yourself unconditionally first and foremost – which is all the more important in a world where we are bombarded with the idea of perfection through advertising, film, television and social media.

We may only have several people whom we can say we love unconditionally — people we have in our energy field or aura, which is intrinsically linked to our higher self. They are the ones we trust implicitly, whom we give our unconditional love to and show our authentic nature to. Sometimes we might feel challenged or threatened by how these people behave, but when we love them unconditionally we respond according to how we would want to be treated by others. This way we diffuse the situation in a loving way. It does not mean, however, that we allow our loved ones to take advantage of our loving nature; it simply means we can choose how to respond so that we always stay true to our nature and honour what our loved one is going through.

Unconditional love is giving love to another without expecting reward and accepting them for all that they are, their limitations included, without wanting to change them. Unconditional love does not, however, mean that you should tolerate controlling behaviour, which is returned as conditioned love. If this is the case, then you are free to remove yourself from the relationship and find a better relationship that allows you to give unconditional love in a safe and healthy way.

Likewise, if you try to be someone you aren't and behave unauthentically in order to receive love then this is based on conditioned love. Your angels of love encourage you to love yourself unconditionally in order that you love others unconditionally, and you will then receive unconditional love in return.

Unconditional love in your energy field

Love is different with everyone you form a relationship with, and even though you love certain people in your life, you may not necessarily love them all unconditionally. This can simply be because they are loved ones, family members or friends whom you trust but have a certain element of reserve towards, or perhaps you feel you can't reveal your full authentic self when you're around them. This is not deception; it's just a different love that sets boundaries. You still care very deeply for these people, but they are not as close to you as those whom you love unconditionally. By recognising this, you place these people in another energy field outside your aura, which separates the two.

Then there are people you love and cherish and care about deeply, who open up a certain side of you, but with whom you perhaps don't spend as much time or share as much of who you are. These you place in another energy field around the second, so that you now have two further spheres of energy around your auric field containing all those you care about. By defining your different relationships and separating them from those you love unconditionally, you set your boundaries within your relationships.

Outside of those spheres you have what I refer to as the 'outer hemisphere', and this is where you place people such as associates, colleagues, neighbours and friends — and they are mixed in with all of humanity. When we recognise that hemisphere as containing people we care about and respect then it helps us to also connect with and care about all people on this planet, whatever their age, background, religion, sex or beliefs.

Having an awareness of these different energy fields also allows us to set boundaries so that we don't allow people into our 'inner sanctum' who do not treat us well. And it gives us the power to move people in and out of our energy fields, depending on how the relationship dynamic changes. If, for instance, someone we love unconditionally in our aura does something that betrays us so deeply that we can no longer trust them, we may not be able to banish them from our life — if they're a family member, for example. However, when we have set our boundaries and trust that our angels of love will protect us, we have the power to move them energetically to whichever sphere makes us feel safe. This does not remove the pain of the situation, but it helps us to heal in time and to re-establish the boundaries that stabilise us. You may, therefore, not have to move that family member out of your life altogether; you may be able to move them to the third or outer energy field and still be able to love them to a degree. And that person should feel the change in energy, too, and respect your decision, hopefully learning from the situation and maybe even making the necessary changes to create another level of love that will serve you both in the future.

This is not giving in and letting people do what they want to you, but letting them know that you forgive their limitations and bad behaviour and have used loving disallowance to put yourself first and send a powerful message to the other person: that you love them but will not tolerate their misbehaviour. By doing this, you are being true to yourself.

Loving someone unconditionally is not just about the happy times; it can often create discomfort. It does not mean that you protect them from these uncomfortable situations. Often, as parents, we have to let our children go through fearful experiences or make tough decisions in order to learn and grow. This is all part of the maturing process. Allowing them to learn about failure is just as important, if not more so, as learning about success in order to help them navigate their own lives.

The real test of unconditional love is when someone is hurtful towards you. It may well be that they don't feel unconditional love for themselves, or that you have reflected back to them something that they want to change in themselves. For whatever reason, they have revealed it to you, and it's for you to decide how to deal with it. When you love someone unconditionally despite their behaviour, it allows you to see them without judgement. By showing love to that person you are being non-reactionary and shining love back at them, so that they can see the love they have within them if they so choose. You cannot be hurt by doing this, as your angels of love are always protecting you. Only when you choose to respond with fear or negativity do you disconnect from your angels, so it goes without saying: keep aligned, respond with unconditional love and you will always have your angels of love there to guide you.

You can show unconditional love even to those in your outer hemisphere by performing small acts of kindness every day to complete strangers: give way to cars, allow someone to move in front of you in a queue, help someone who's lost or give some small change to a homeless person on the street. Giving unconditionally to strangers and expecting nothing in return sends a powerful energy of love into the outer hemisphere, which has a knock-on effect on all those who reside there (i.e. the rest of humanity). One kind gesture to a stranger every day has a ripple effect that is far-reaching and goes towards making our world a more loving and peaceful place.

Unconditional love un-limits our life experience. Harold W. Becker, who wrote *Unconditional Love: An Unlimited Way of Being*, explores the realms of unlimited possibility by being open to choosing a new way of thinking, feeling and being. He suggests that when we truly accept all that we are through our limitations, beliefs, mistakes and misunderstandings, we honour our self-worth, value our capabilities and give ourselves permission to be authentic. In turn, this releases us from what we feel others expect of us. We then have the ability to see who we really are through others.

When we love unconditionally, it changes how we think and behave, and turns hope into confidence that anything can be achieved or overcome.

In the great British writer C. S. Lewis's book *The Four Loves*, he explores the four different kinds of human love. He includes affection, which he defines as the most basic of all the loves; friendship, the rarest but most perceptive of all the loves; passionate love, which he deems the most expansive and profound form, ranging from bliss to the ability to feel suicidal; and finally the love of God — the greatest, most charitable and least selfish form.

We humans reside here on earth alongside the animals, and these three kingdoms are designed to work in harmony together. As the dominant kingdom, humans have free will and the ability to make choices towards ourselves, our fellow man, the earth and animal kingdoms, but, on the whole, we also have an understanding that we reside on this beautiful planet and ought to love it and all that exist on it, unconditionally. It is only when we are ignorant of this that we inflict harm on Mother Earth.

When we truly learn to love our planet unconditionally, that's when we can start to reverse the damage that's been caused up until now. When we become aware that we are all part of the same energy soup and have unconditional love and respect for our world, it is said that we go into a state of 'eutierria' — a feeling of oneness with the earth and its life forces.

Mother Earth has a predisposition for unconditional love, but it's only when we fully reciprocate that we understand what this glorious planet is teaching us about ourselves. Scientific experiments have proved that plants are affected by our thoughts and words (see page 33), and that plant extracts can affect our mental state in return (see page 120).

Often plants can also give an indication of whether a home is hostile or loving. House plants will pick up the thoughts, words and feelings of those in the home, so if your plants suffer and don't survive, look at whether there is regular hostility in the home among those living there.

Pets, too, can teach us so much about unconditional love and loyalty. Even if they've done something wrong and been scolded, they will still show love and affection without harbouring any resentment or misgivings. Again, experiments have been conducted to prove how stress-reducing and healing pets can be, as they stimulate the alpha frequency in us, the frequency of calm, which stimulates our higher self and enables us to go into a loving state. Having pets can aid healing, alleviate conditions such as depression and offer companionship, taking us out of isolation and into loving relationships.

My father had a dog when he was a young boy and each day his dog would walk with him to the end of the road where they lived and watch as my father walked off to school. The dog would return home to the house for the day, and no matter what time my father returned in the afternoon, the dog would know and walk to the end of the road to meet him.

Renowned biologist Rupert Sheldrake writes in his amazing book *The Sense of Being Stared at: and Other Aspects of the Extended Mind* about the intricacies of the mind and how we're able to communicate not only with one another through our inner senses, but also with animals. His experiments show that we have so much more ability than we realise to communicate through our higher selves, and that when we learn to communicate on a more intuitive level (which is connected to the right side of our brain, our heart and consciousness) we can create a more loving world.

His experiments put pets and their owners, who are linked by unconditional love, into controlled situations whereby the owners are placed in a room on the third floor of a house and the dogs are placed on the ground floor. The owners are then asked to think that they are speaking to their dog and suggesting they go for a walk, and the dogs will pick up on this and react, despite not even being in the same room.

Many people have similarly recorded how pets have reacted when their owners have died, while pet owners will often tell you that they feel their pets were gifted to them, as they have made such an impact on their lives, becoming part of the family and teaching them so much about embracing unconditional love. Intuitively connected to us through the heart, our pets pick up on our thoughts and feelings, even when we're not with them. The animal and earth kingdoms have been showing us for millennia how to overcome our limitations as human beings by loving unconditionally, and our angels of love always encourage us to connect with both kingdoms, especially to spend time in nature. It is up to us, however, to respect, accept and appreciate their message of just how capable we are of reaching our full and glorious potential by learning how to love.

Simon came to me at a time in his life when his career as a policeman had really challenged him, the love of his life had left him and his world had fallen apart. He'd suffered a serious injury on a job when he tried to apprehend someone who was driving off in a car and, as the car sped off, his arm was wrenched. Simon had treatment for his injury, but it didn't heal well and this caused him to become depressed, and it finally affected his relationship. Desperate for answers, he was seeing signs everywhere he went, especially in coded form in car registration plates, so he came to see me to help him find a resolution and to understand what the messages meant.

I introduced Simon to his angels of love, who started to come to him in dreams and visions to help him work on self-love, and despite his hopes that his lost love would return, slowly but surely he started to feel better and to attract people and situations that would help him find his best self again.

One day, he was the first officer to arrive at the hospital bedside of a young woman who'd been involved in a horrific assault that left her with noticeable scars for life. He was there for her during a time when she was going through incredible pain and suffering and was involved in putting a case together to prosecute the person who had committed the heinous crime. Simon realised that his angels of love had guided him to be involved in that case, as it had opened his heart to such a degree that it changed him for life.

He finally recognised that he had never known his full capacity to love until that experience. It had introduced him to an understanding of acceptance, non-judgement and many facets of love that he had never even touched on before in his relationships. And while he'd thought he'd lost the love of his life, he realised as he grew that he was only feeling conditioned love, as he had been focusing on what that relationship meant to him.

Eventually he made the choice to leave the force with the guidance of his angels of love, which helped him to fully recover physically and mentally from his accident. He met a beautiful woman who became his life partner, his love of life returned and his relationships all deepened as a result of him discovering his ability to love unconditionally.

Prayer to attract unconditional love

This prayer is for attracting unconditional love into your life in all ways. Say this last thing at night when you're in bed. Sitting upright, take some deep breaths until you are calm and relaxed, then say the following:

Dear angels of love who guide and protect me,
   I call upon you to hear my prayer. Help me to open my heart to give and receive unconditional love. Help me learn

how to grow in order to expand my capacity to love and receive love. Help me not to shy away through fear of getting hurt, but to trust that I will always be protected by your guidance as long as my heart stays open and I remain true to my higher self, if it be for the highest good of all.

Amen

Your light bulb moment

Use this exercise whenever you have any doubts, fears or uncertainty and you wish to check if your heart energy centre is open and you are ready to embrace life fully with acceptance and unconditional love. You can do this using a pendulum, but if you don't have one, you can use your body instead.

1. First, set your pendulum, or body, by asking your angels of love to show you how it will move for a 'yes' answer. Gently start a swaying motion with your pendulum or your body and then just relax and see which way it moves. Your pendulum may swing clockwise, anti-clockwise or up and down. Whichever way it swings, record this as your 'yes' answer. Your body, however, will move forward and back or side to side. Again, record which way your body naturally moves to record your 'yes' answer.

2. Repeat the above to check for your 'no' answer.

3. Once you have your 'yes' and 'no' answers set, ask your angels of love to help you see if your heart energy centre is open.

4. If the answer is yes, then thank your angels of love for showing you, but if your answer is no, ask your angels of love, *'What is going on for me right now?'* Listen carefully as your angels of love can answer you through your thoughts and feelings. If you don't get anything straight away, ask your angels, *'Please show me, when the time is right, why my heart energy centre is not fully open.'* Trust that they will show you and be open and willing to receive their messages and insight.

5. When your angels of love have shown you what the reason is, ask them, *'Angels of love, please show me what I need to do to open my heart once more.'* Again, you may get an immediate response, but if not, repeat, *'Please show me, when the time is right, what I need to do to open my heart energy centre fully.'*

Our heart can sometimes close when life challenges us, but always know that your angels of love will be there to help you open it so that you remain true to your higher self. You will then be able to give and receive unconditional love, and attain your natural state of true harmony and balance.

Chapter summary

Unconditional love is an expression of our higher self. It gives us freedom, peace and an increased awareness that allows us to fully engage with life and relationships. When we learn how to love unconditionally in all ways — whether it's the planet, animal life or our fellow man — it opens us to limitless possibilities and attracts people and experiences that will fulfil our desires and potential. By loving in this way, we honour our whole self and become aligned to the oneness of life, creating peace and harmony between ourselves and the people we come into contact with, our environment and the world at large.

COUNT YOUR BLESSINGS

Why do you feel blessed today . . .?

....

....

....

....

....

....

....

....

....

....

....

....

....

....

....

....

....

7

Soul Mates, Twin Flames and Life Partners

Your heart ignites my essence,
Your eyes reveal your soul,
When apart, we're still complete,
Eternal, wise and whole.

We attract certain types of relationships depending on our needs during certain stages of our life, as relationships are always about serving one another's needs. Often, we recognise that some of our relationships can involve intensive lesson-learning and can sometimes be life-changing. There are many facets to relationships, but it's interesting to look at soul mates, twin flames and life partners, as these have the biggest impact on us.

When we ask our angels of love to help us attract a partner, we will be guided to one who serves our highest needs at that time, even though we may look back in hindsight and wonder what we were being shown when the relationship hasn't worked out. Sometimes we can't see straight away what the point of the relationship was. I've certainly looked back on some and wondered, but I have then gone on to recognise the lesson later, when the time was right. Our angels of love know everything about us: our past, present and future selves.

Take a look below and see if any of these types of relationship have played out in your own life, either currently or in the past:

Soul mates

There can sometimes be a misconception that soul mates are for life, but you don't necessarily have just one soul-mate relationship in your life. Soul mates are for growth, for life lessons and to help you become a better version of yourself. They can be romantic partners, but they can also be friends or family, too.

Soul mates share a deep connection and resonate in a 'knowing' or intuitive joining together of souls, which enriches both parties and allows them to work towards a higher state of awareness. Often soul mates feel they've known each other before, or just have an affinity with one another. While each person feels they can be truly alive and authentic with the other, these relationships do come with their challenges, as each person mirrors the other's flaws.

Soul mates can arrive in your life unexpectedly and often do so when growth is required. The connection between soul mates is often from an emotional perspective, with no words needed. Much of the communication is through body language and feelings, so when two people come together in unison it's a journey of growth as well as commitment to one another. Soul mates can be for life, but you don't choose them; they are magnetically drawn to you so that you both reap the benefits of the relationship, whether it's fleeting or for life.

Twin flames

Twin flames are similar to soul mates, in that they are there to help with our soul's growth, though they are recognised by some experts as occurring when a soul evolves to a certain level and then splits in two. If you've met your twin flame in the past or are with that person now, it is like looking in a mirror. These are usually very intense relationships and may not work if you both have unresolved issues. They can spark growth for you both, though not necessarily together. They tend to be romantic in nature or deep friendships.

As twin flames mirror one another, they can be very in tune, having the same interests, thinking the same thoughts and even sharing the same dreams. Twin flames are magnetically pulled towards one another, so physical attraction is usually a key part of the relationship.

As this type of relationship can reveal deep issues within both partners, the experience may be life-changing. If both people in the relationship have worked on themselves then they will grow through self-awareness; if not, however, this can create conflict, as each person finds their own weaknesses and faults reflected back at them. As twin flames share a soul, it can only exist authentically, therefore only a true version of each person can make this type of relationship work. Consequently, though beautiful and rich in lesson-learning, twin-flame relationships do not tend to make lifelong partnerships.

I remember the day I met my twin flame face to face. We had met under unusual circumstances and for many weeks had spoken only on the phone through a work situation, but from the moment we first spoke it was as if I was speaking to my other half, and he felt it, too. Try as I might to stop meeting this man, the draw to him was incredibly intense and, in the end, we had to both find out why the pull was so strong.

For many months we met, stunned by our similarities in looks, tastes and interests. We were also both going through relationship splits at the time with our partners, and while we respected those situations and tried to keep one another at arm's length, it was challenging and often painful to be apart. It was evident from the outset that we had found each other in order to go through an immense shift in our higher awareness.

Our lives changed completely as we both started to evolve and discover new aspects of ourselves, but equally, as we both mirrored back to one another our weaknesses, it became inevitable that our relationship would come to an abrupt halt. And sure enough, it ended almost as dramatically as it had begun. My heartache was profound, but that relationship ignited my blueprint and drove me to discover my innate self. I'm truly grateful for my twin flame and all he taught me, and if you've ever had this incredible experience yourself then you may well recognise the growth and expansiveness of feeling that can come from that connection.

Life partners

Life partners arrive in your life when you're ready for unconditional love, support and shared commitment. Because they're there with you for the long haul, they will have similar interests to you but will equally encourage you to take risks in life in order to better yourself. They will put you first and foremost, and not consider what works best for them. Whereas soul mates and twin flames can conjure up many issues and power struggles between them, life partners have a truly unconditionally loving relationship.

Life partners can be soul mates or twin flames as well, but only if their souls' growth has reached that state of completion that allows for a sustainable lifelong commitment to one another. Life partners have evolved to a state of worthiness and self-love, which makes for a far more peaceful and harmonic relationship. They often come from different backgrounds, which means they must both learn about the other person's world and each will feel their love develop during that journey. The differences between them create a rich bed of curiosity that feeds the relationship and keeps the fire in their hearts burning for eternity.

Life partners are driven primarily by their intellectual connection, and even though their mutual passion is discernible, it is far more likely that the bedrock of the relationship is based on mental stimulation rather than emotional, creating more stability.

Your life partner will appear in your life when you are ready for a more harmonious way of life. And because they are able to live more in the present, instead of bringing up past issues, they make good marriage partners.

Ron and Kim became clients of mine some years ago when Kim initiated contact with me. She recognised that they were experiencing challenges in their lives that were related to their health. Both were self-employed with their own respective businesses, and they found the pressure and the long hours were reflecting other issues in their lives.

After a few sessions with Kim alone, Ron finally agreed to come and see me as well. It was evident that Ron was very intuitive, but also very open to negative energies because of the nature of his role as a caregiver. As a result of his previous work in a hospice, he had a tendency to see and hear things that disturbed him, and in order to find out what was attracting these experiences, he came to see if he could find the answers.

Ron was very open to meeting his angels of love during his healing sessions with me. It was apparent that he was dealing with ill health, but his stoic attitude overrode his concerns as he battled on through with life.

Finally, after a few months of working with Kim initially and then Ron, I became aware that there was a depth of love between the two of them that was affected by karma. Ron and Kim had met briefly before but then bumped into one another one day in the street and decided to have a coffee together. Kim invited Ron to do some gardening for her and although Ron was married (albeit unhappily), he turned up to work for her that day and never left.

They instantly knew they were life partners, and Ron soon moved in with Kim. While they initially faced challenges adapting to one another's lives and detaching themselves from what had held them back in the past, their love for one another was steeped in the knowledge that theirs was a lifelong commitment. When they met me their souls were still growing, and so in the initial stages I was helping their soul-mate relationship reach a level of maturity.

Finally, Ron and Kim recognised that their work and the other aspects of their lives that frustrated them no longer mattered so much, and although Kim became unwell herself for a time, the love and commitment to her recovery that came from Ron was unconditional and beautiful. Their relationship evolved and their lives eventually reflected a new level of commitment as life partners.

Great loves that have shaped history

Antony and Cleopatra
Probably one of the most famous of all relationships in history was that of Cleopatra VII, Queen of Egypt, and Roman General

Marcus Antonius in 41 BC. Octavian, Julius Caesar's adopted son, was in dispute at the time with Mark Antony over the Roman leadership after Caesar had been assassinated.

Cleopatra, known for her shrewdness and powers of seduction, began a romantic and political relationship with Mark Antony. They had three children together.

In 31 BC, Cleopatra and Mark Antony united their armies against Octavian in the mighty Battle of Actium but were overpowered, so they escaped back to the protection of Egypt. A year later, however, Octavian overpowered the Egyptian capital Alexandria, where the couple had fled, and when Mark Antony's own army deserted him, he took his own life.

On 12 August in 30 BC, Cleopatra locked herself and two female servants into her bed chamber and also committed suicide. She was buried with Mark Antony as a sign of her lifelong commitment to him, while Octavian went on to rule Egypt.

Henry VIII and Anne Boleyn

The story of King Henry VIII's relationship with Anne Boleyn, his second wife of six, in the sixteenth century was one of seduction and enchantment, but it ended in betrayal and murder so that he could love another. Despite how brief their intense love affair was, it was said to have changed England from a Catholic to a Protestant nation.

As Henry's first wife Catherine of Aragon was unsuccessful in giving him a male heir, his eye for the ladies turned towards Anne, who was one of the queen's ladies-in-waiting. It was not Anne's beauty he was drawn to but her intelligence and wit. However, Anne was reluctant to be seduced by the king unless he promised to marry her, so Henry asked Pope Clement VII for an annulment to his marriage to Catherine. The pope refused.

Breaking free of the Roman Catholic Church, Henry made himself head of the Church of England and arranged for his marriage to Catherine to be annulled. He secretly married Anne Boleyn in 1533. Although historians claim there were a number of reasons why England transformed into a Protestant nation, they also believe that this romance was a major catalyst for this change.

Soon, however, the king tired of waiting for a son and heir from Anne and in 1536 he had her arrested and beheaded for witchcraft, incest and adultery, despite the allegations being false. Only eleven days later he married his third wife, Jane Seymour.

Winston and Clementine Churchill

This iconic couple met only briefly in 1904 at a ball, when Winston was said to have been awestruck by Clementine. She, on the other hand, was seemingly unmoved by their meeting. However, four years later when they met again, they were married within four months.

Winston's proposal took place when he invited Clementine to Blenheim Palace, his Oxfordshire birthplace. While walking in the gardens they had to take shelter from the rain in an ornamental Greek temple where, romantically, he then proposed. At the time it was supposed that he would marry Violet Asquith, who was overcome when she heard the news.

Clementine was among the few who could stand up to Winston, a difficult man at times, but their love was clear to everyone. When apart, they would communicate by letter, and even when together in the same house, they would write notes of affection to one another.

Winston relied on Clementine for her loyalty; she supported him through immense challenges and was his advocate, ally and advisor whenever he needed her. Winston famously told Clementine: *'I do not love and never will love any woman in the world but you.'*

Their love is iconic and is believed to have been the bedrock of Winston Churchill's stability throughout his crucial, turbulent years as the British prime minister during the Second World War.

Pierre and Marie Curie
Marie was born in Poland in 1867 and went on to gain a good education, earning degrees in maths and science. She was introduced to Pierre Curie — a French physicist and chemist — in 1894. Though Pierre was eight years older than Marie, the pair were drawn to one another through their similar backgrounds and interests. They married after only knowing one another for a year.

Marie started to research uranium rays — which had recently been discovered by Professor Antoine Henri

Becquerel — for her doctoral thesis and Pierre joined her, and in 1898 the couple discovered two new chemical elements: polonium and radium. Along with Becquerel, the Curies were awarded the Nobel Prize in Physics in 1903 for their pioneering work on radioactivity.

Their first daughter was born in 1898, and their second in 1904, but two years later Pierre was tragically killed in a street accident in Paris, where he worked as the Chair of Physics at the Sorbonne. Marie was heartbroken but dedicated her life to carrying on his work, taking over his role at the Sorbonne and becoming the university's first female professor. After winning another Nobel Prize in 1911, Marie became fascinated with radium's potential to work as a cancer therapy, which guided the focus for the Radium Institute. She sadly died in 1934 from leukaemia after years of exposure to radioactive substances.

Irene, Marie and Pierre's daughter, went on to share the Nobel Prize in 1935 with her husband for discovering artificial radioactivity, having carried on the family tradition. Today Marie Curie is a charitable organisation in the UK that supports people with terminal illnesses and their families.

Mildred and Richard Loving

Mildred Jeter and Richard Loving met and fell in love when they were teenagers, but as Richard was a white man and Mildred was of African and Native American parentage, they were not allowed to marry in their home state of Virginia due to anti-miscegenation laws, which made interracial relationships illegal.

In 1958, they drove eighty miles away to Washington DC to exchange their vows in a ceremony, only to be arrested five weeks later for breaking the law. Although the Lovings showed the officers their marriage certificate, they were told by the officers that it was not valid in the Commonwealth and in 1959 they pleaded guilty to *'cohabiting as man and wife, against the peace and dignity of the Commonwealth'*.

They were sentenced to one year in prison and banned from visiting their home state of Virginia for twenty-five years. In 1964 Mildred wrote to Attorney General Robert F. Kennedy, who then referred their appeal to the American Civil Liberties Union. They were represented by lawyers who volunteered to take their case to the Supreme Court, and in 1967 a landmark verdict in the case of Loving v. Virginia ruled in favour of the Lovings, unanimously overturning the bans on interracial marriage in Virginia and across the US.

The Lovings stayed in Virginia and had three children, but in 1975 Richard was sadly killed in a car crash. Mildred remained in the house that Richard had built her until she died in 2008.

This couple knew no bounds when it came to expressing their love. They not only stood up to the judiciary against injustice, but left a lasting legacy of diversity and equality in our communities that continues to this day.

These iconic relationships are examples of those whose love has had a far-reaching influence on generations throughout history. Love is a power that can create positive change within families, communities and the world at large. We have all met a couple whose relationship is profound and makes an impact. This is what love can do when two people push past their fears and limitations and allow their love to guide them. Our angels of love are there to help us in all our relationships, regardless of the seeming limitations. Calling upon their assistance makes this a better world for us all to live in.

Affirmations to attract the love that you need in your life now

If you want to attract a new love into your life or bring renewed love into a current relationship, say these affirmations to your angels of love first thing in the morning as you wake and last thing at night before you sleep, for thirty days:

Angels of love,

I love myself unconditionally and therefore attract unconditional love back to me in all ways.

My home is a place of unconditional love, peace and tranquillity.

My relationship with my partner is authentic and unconditional, based on the life lessons we're here to learn, and I embrace them wholeheartedly with acceptance, love and grace.

161

I always attract loving relationships in daily life so that my soul can grow.

Watch for any changes or improvements in your current relationship or be aware of any new relationships you attract into your life. Make notes in your journal as you embrace the changes that your angels of love are helping you to make and see.

Your light bulb moment

Use these exercises to encourage a new relationship into your life or improve your current relationship and prepare the way for its arrival:

Prepare a space
Declutter your room and prepare it, ready to welcome someone new into your personal space or to share the love that you both deserve in your current relationship (see page 98).

Set your intention
Find a quiet time, light a candle and then write down how you want to live your life with your ideal partner, including all the attributes, thoughts and feelings you are looking for. Place this note by your bedside with a piece of rose quartz and know that your angels of love will receive your request.

Chapter summary

Soul mates, twin flames and life partners have a greater influence on our soul's growth, depending on what our higher self needs in that moment. We will attract the relationships that best serve us at the time, so although those relationships can be challenging when we meet aspects of ourselves we don't like, we must accept that this is only for our highest good. Some of these relationships may not last as long as we would expect or hope, but in hindsight, when we've come through the experience, we will be able to see what the purpose of them was if we ask our angels of love for their insight.

COUNT YOUR BLESSINGS

Why do you feel blessed today...?

....

....

....

....

....

....

....

....

....

....

....

....

....

....

....

....

....

....

8

Love Makes the World Go Around

Love creates our glory,
It changes history,
A paradox we all go through,
An enchanting mystery.

Love is the prerequisite for a procreative, productive and harmonic society and a respect for all living creatures on our planet. It is the greatest power of all, which as humans we learn to understand through recognising unconditional love as the ultimate of all loves.

Throughout history, love has been explored, researched and expressed through art, literature and song. Humans have endeavoured ceaselessly to experience love through their external senses while experiencing the whole spectrum of love through their inner senses. History has shown us how it's shaped our world: nations have been created through the love of their people and some of those nations have come and gone. The same can be said of different religions that have risen and fallen while proclaiming the path to true love. Above all, it is not something that has been invented or created by man; it comes from Source itself. It's connected to each and every one of us and we need only reach within ourselves to discover our capabilities and learn how to uncover the marvel of love's various aspects, and unconditional love in particular. Our angels of love are there every step of the way, whenever we need their assistance, to make the very best of our existence on this earth.

Learning how to love ourselves and others and how to allow others to love us, teaches us to respect all as if they were our mothers, fathers, brothers, sisters, sons or daughters. When we fully embrace this concept, we have reached a level of awareness and wisdom akin to the teachings from our spiritual forefathers.

When we lived in small, simple communities, we worked in harmony and love for the greatest good of our people. We relied on self-love and love of our community to survive, working from a higher perspective, so as to be aware of what actions would help support those in need or bring the group dynamic back into alignment.

Working naturally with the biorhythms of the earth, with plant life and animal life, our forefathers would have had unconditional love and respect for everything, so that it all worked and evolved in loving harmony together.

The young, the old, the sick, the healthy — or whoever was part of that dynamic — was loved as a small cog in a larger machine. No one was excluded unless they were extradited for the greater good of the community. When we love unconditionally, we also have to take into account using loving disallowance when necessary so that equilibrium is maintained.

The three forms of yogic love

Yogic tradition teaches that there are three kinds of love. The first is absolute love, Source, which is connected to everything, including our angels of love. Our messengers are constantly encouraging us to understand this.

The second is individual love, which is born of our personality and with which we attract others to us. Our angels of love constantly help us to navigate the intricate challenges that these relationships create for us.

The third is our practice and our attitudes towards ourselves and others. Our angels of love guide us to learn lessons and to form good habits and behaviours that reflect back through our relationship with ourselves, others and our environment.

When we learn to understand all three, we grow as individuals and fully embrace the enormity of what we can achieve through love in all its forms. That's when we create a better life for ourselves and the world around us.

The seven forms of Greek love

According to the Ancient Greeks, there are seven kinds of love, which are as follows:

Eros

According to Greek myth, Eros — the god of love and desire — fired arrows into the hearts of mortals and immortals, which was said to have brought on a form of madness. This is the love associated with what we know today as romantic love, although the Greeks felt this was the most dangerous form of all, as it led to the most difficulties and challenges.

Philia

This is the love of friendship and of the mind. This is based on platonic love, which the Greeks deemed far more invaluable than Eros love. Interestingly, Aristotle said that friendships are formed for three reasons: because the person is useful to us, pleasant and, mostly, good. When friendships are created on the basis of goodness, there is a mutual benefit to both parties through trust, dependability and companionship. Plato felt that the best kind of friendship was one born out of romantic love, as that link would in turn strengthen and develop the relationship further, allowing it to transcend a desire for ownership to become a wish for morality.

Real friendships are the basis for authenticity and will teach each partner about their limitations in order to grow together.

Ludus

Ludus is the playful or non-committed kind of love. This is usually experienced in the early stages of romantic love, when flirting, teasing and seduction take place, but it can also lead to a no-strings-attached kind of encounter. This is the type of relationship that is casual, unchallenging and simple, and while it often may not lead to a long-term committed relationship, it can turn out to be long-lasting. It's the kind of relationship that works when two people are self-aware, emotionally mature and don't want to form roots together. It only gets complicated if one in the relationship thinks Ludus is Eros, but Ludus is in actual fact far more compatible with Philia.

Storge

This is akin to familial love, such as parents have for their children. This love is effortless and natural. It understands sacrifice, acceptance and forgiveness. It is a kind of Philia, which is created from dependency, but unlike Eros or Philia it is not attracted through our personal qualities. Sometimes people who are in the early stages of Eros expect unconditional love born of Storge, but are disappointed when they only experience the needy and dependent side of Storge. However, if this is a life-partner or soul-mate relationship and given time, it will mature through Philia and Eros and eventually into Storge.

Agape

This is the love for humanity, the universal love and acceptance of all, including our planet and all who reside on it. This is the love of unselfishness and the love for others, which is all about acceptance and unconditional love. It is born of empathy for others and connects us to our fellow man. It is the very substance that sustains our society and enriches our communities, encouraging us to be better people while empowering others to better themselves and our planet.

Pragma

This is a love of practicality, usually through a feeling of duty. An example of Pragma is arranged marriages, which still occur today. Some relationships that start off as Eros or Ludus can end up as a combination of Storge and Pragma. Shared goals and personal qualities tend to take precedence over sexual attraction in this love and as such it is deemed the highest form of love, characterised by commitment, understanding and tolerance. This comes from two people knowing each other deeply over many years.

Philautia

This is self-love, and therefore governs whether we are healthy or unhealthy. In Ancient Greece, a person would be deemed hubristic if they considered themselves above the gods or the greater good. Today, hubris can be interpreted as ego, an inflated sense of one's self, abilities and accomplishments. Hubris is known as the creator of injustice, hostility and struggle. However, healthy self-love is an awareness of one's self in relation to others and the greater good. People with healthy Philautia do not need props, they are not dependent on others or destructive influences and do not fear failure or rejection. They react to pain as we all do, but they are not inhibited or hurt by challenge; they grow from it.

When we make love our daily mantra, as opposed to fear, we open up to a world of potential, which is good for our health and mental wellbeing. It boosts our creativity, relationships and productivity and ultimately helps us to achieve our goals and pass on positive programmes to future generations. When we react to challenges in our lives in ways that can lead to drama, it renders us limited and disconnected from our angels of love and, above all, from Source. Every challenge is an opportunity to ask our angels of love to show us the lesson that will help us grow and find the right solution that will instil in us eternal love directly from Source.

Love is all around us at every given moment, but it is our choice whether we hide from it, fear it or miss the opportunities we have to reach a greater understanding of it. If, on the other hand, we embrace it, we are sure to find compassion and a deeper peace within our lives and loves.

Prayer to help make this a better world

This prayer is for Agape, the love of humanity. Use it to call upon your angels of love who will help you with growth, love and compassion for yourself, your loved ones, your friends, your community and your fellow human beings. This form of love will connect you to your purpose, your true power, your right people and your place in this world to bring ultimate fulfilment through a sense of selflessness, empathy and authenticity to your higher self.

Use this prayer to connect with your angels of love last thing at night, just before you sleep.

Dear angels of love who guide and protect me,

I accept unconditionally the love that you give me from Source.

I accept that your love is ever present within and all around me.

If I have held back through fear, please show me how to open my heart to all of humanity, as this is my deepest desire.

Please help me to always welcome opportunities, even when I feel vulnerable and doubt my capabilities.

Please release me from all that holds me back from seeing and fully experiencing the love that's all around me.

Let me learn how to let go of judgement and embrace acceptance with grace.

Let me be open to receiving signs from you in all ways through my inner sight, hearing and feelings, so that I may be aligned to your messages of truth.

I give myself full permission to see love in all ways.

I give myself full permission to hear love in all ways.

I give myself full permission to feel love in all ways.

I give myself full permission to give and receive love in all ways and to experience the whole spectrum of love unconditionally in all its glory.

Thank you, dear angels of love, for always reminding me that I am love.

And it is so.

Amen

Your light bulb moment

Past, present and future angel card reading

If you don't have a deck of angel cards, now is perhaps the time to choose one for your own personal use. If you have several, choose a pack that you would like to use as your daily deck.

Choose three cards from your chosen deck of angel cards each morning as part of your practice to see what you may need to know for your day. Make sure you shuffle them first, then place each of the three cards you have chosen face down in front of you and ask your angels of love to reveal to you through the words and pictures what it is you need to know right now in order to help you with your love of self, relationships and humanity. When you feel ready to receive your message from your angels, turn the cards over, from left to right, to reveal their insights.

Your left card reveals the past, the centre card the present and the card on your right is your future. Looking at all three, you may be able to read a message instantly, or you may well want to take your time to see what each one is trying to show you. All three are linked, however, so your angels of love will be encouraging you to see what you need to know in the present, as well as how that is connected to your past and, of course, how that will affect your future.

Make a note in your journal of what you feel your angels are communicating to you, thank your angels for their message of love and honour the message you've received, either by accepting what you've learned or, if action is necessary, making a note of what your angels are encouraging you to do.

This exercise can be repeated every day in order to learn any necessary lessons or to reveal what you perhaps can't see but your angels want you to address. Your angels of love will always guide you for your highest good.

Chapter summary

When we understand that love is all around us, in each and every living thing, and that it is constantly there for us to embrace, we can learn to grow through its many facets until we come to a place of loving respect and humility for our fellow man and the planet. We are each but one small cog in a maze of perpetual loving motion, moving and expanding, creating and healing all that we are, all that we were and all that we can be. When we truly understand the breadth of our capacity to love, we have the ability to share that love for the greater good of all to make this a better world to live in.

COUNT YOUR BLESSINGS

Why do you feel blessed today...?

....

....

....

....

....

....

....

....

....

....

....

....

....

....

....

....

....

....

A Note from the Author

When my publisher announced they were ready for me to write this second book in the *Talking with Angels* series, I thought, *Oh no, here we go again. What am I going to go through this time?* Especially as this book was about angels of love. I knew in a heartbeat that I was about to dive into a period of great challenge, as had happened before when I wrote *Talking with Angels of Light.* During that time, I was plagued with ill health and, having gone through a huge amount of loss, my world was starting to fall apart around me. But my angels of light kept me focused during the writing of that first book and allowed me to see its true purpose. It was as if they were reminding me that, no matter what, I would get through it all. After all, that was the essence of what the book was all about!

As the book started to take shape, so did my life. Not only did I manage to make a full recovery, but I rebuilt my life anew based on a deeper relationship with my angels, who showed me with unwavering faith that the book was a source of healing for me. Their light shone brighter than ever as I found a new level in myself that I hadn't discovered before, a humbleness deeper than I'd ever known and a gratitude that held me through times of uncertainty, until finally, as the book was completed, so was my transformation.

It's akin to the chicken or the egg scenario. Which came first? Was my situation created so that, when I wrote the first book, it could reflect back to me the messages that would remind me how to aid my own transformation? We are never at a point in our lives where we think we've got there. As soon as we think we know it all, have achieved all we need to achieve and attained what we feel we need, we realise we are fooling ourselves.

For example, I used to strive to get to a point in my life where I was financially stable. I had a good home, good relationships and felt secure, yet these weren't really the things I wanted. As soon as I faced adversity, the very process of overcoming that adversity revealed to me the 'truth' of what I really wanted to achieve — and it wasn't the logical, simple ticking-off-the-list things that I thought would make me happy.

In fact, the more I wanted these things, the more they eluded me. So when I look back at what came first, the chicken or the egg, I realise that actually the book was given to me so that even when I lost everything through illness, I could create something beautiful out of my misfortune . . . and I did. As my angels communicated to me what they wanted me to share with my readers, I was actually discovering another aspect of myself and learning that I could reveal what was deeply resonating with me at the time.

So as expected, while writing this book I have had some incredibly testing challenges with relationships. After everything I've learned, I thought I had cracked the 'relationship' and 'love' lessons, but during this process, I realised I was wrong. I experienced an array of self-reflections and had to face difficulties with those I love that I never thought I would have to go through again. From it, however, I've grown, and while there were days when I wanted to give up and hide away from the world, because the encounters just seemed too much to bear, each time I asked my angels of love to guide me they helped me pull through.

This is the third book I've written that has had such a deeply profound effect on me and has helped me through a personal transformation, so I hope that now you've read *Talking with Angels of Love*, it has touched you, too, brought you and your angels of love together in a deeper way and shown you how much love you can bring into your life. Maybe you've even experienced a transformation of your own. Deepening your relationship with your angels of love will always lead you to discover a deeper love of yourself, of life and of those around you. I've certainly achieved that these past few months . . . and I feel I've only just begun this part of my journey.

I can honestly say that I've had some disastrous experiences in relationships throughout my life, but I've had many incredibly beautiful ones, too. I've given my all even when it wasn't welcomed or respected. I've loved when I wasn't loved in return and I've loved in relationships where I thought my heart would break in two. I have found love in strange and meaningful places and been surprised as it's sneaked up and caught me unawares. I've given love the benefit of the doubt and then felt let down. I've learned hard lessons from the ugliness of what it's shown me, but above all, I've never hidden away from it, or closed my heart to all I have been shown that I can give, because I know that if there's anything I have to offer in this world, it is my ability to love unconditionally, even when it's not pretty, reciprocated, respected or understood.

When I was a young woman, I had no one to show me that there was a volume button on my emotions. All I knew was what my angels of love had shown me as a child, so despite my upbringing, I learned to love the adults around me who hurt and manipulated me, and by loving them no matter what they did, I survived. This was all I knew.

I didn't see the lesson until later. As an adult, when I finally realised that I was allowing myself to be victimised because I was programmed to attract destructive relation-ships, and as I'd learned that you must love, despite being hurt and manipulated, I found that when I removed these unwanted conditionings, self-love naturally emerged. When that part of me finally started to help me find my power and my voice, I was able to discern how to change what I was attracting, leading to a better relationship with myself and others.

I can now say that I am a very lucky woman indeed. Not because I am more fortunate than others, but because I luckily paid attention to my angels of love, who throughout my life have been there to love and protect me, so that today I have wonderful, loving people in my life — all the hard work of letting go of that destructive young woman I used to be has truly paid off. There is always a fine line between allowing our logical, fear-based mind to convince us that a message or sign is just a coincidence and the other side of the coin, when we truly pay attention to our angels of love and honour what they've shown us.

So, when I look back at the fifty-two years I've been on this earth, I can wholeheartedly say that every time I've paid attention to the thousands of messages from my angels something positive has come of it. Can I call that a coincidence? No, of course not. Even scientists will tell you that if something keeps giving good results, there must be something to it.

I hadn't realised I had it in me to be as courageous as I have been. I've had to face things that were ugly, raw and at times excessive, to the point of complete emotional meltdown, but throughout the writing of this book my angels of love have reminded me repeatedly, 'You know you will get through this, Amanda. You always do. And you will not only see the lesson, you will understand what you will achieve once you honour what you need to do right now.'

Often, the things I needed to do and say took me completely out of my comfort zone, but each time I went into my heart and asked my angels for assistance I knew that, no matter how scary it was, I would come out the other side. And I did!

So, has this book been helpful to you? I know that writing it has yet again completely changed my perspective on what I thought I was capable of in my relationships with myself and with others, and I hope it has done the same for you. My angels of love have shown me another level of loving that I didn't think was possible, and, despite the hardships, I am grateful for the lessons I've learned, as they have opened up a whole new experience to me that I'm only just beginning to live now.

I hope that, if you've been touched by sorrow and pain and have shied away from it, this book has shown you that your angels of love have your back. Not only will they guide and protect you, they will also love you unconditionally and eternally. By incorporating the practices that they have shared with me to give to you, you will be reminded of this each and every day, and by honouring their insights you will deepen your communication with them always.

Talking with Angels of Love is much more than just an expression of what love is all about. It's an invitation to you from your angels of love to finally allow yourself to fear less and love more.

Our life is filled with treasures
With guidance from above,
Our angels give us all we need
To fill our lives with love.

Invitation to the Reader

I would love you to share your stories with me of how this book has helped you to develop your own angel communication, how it's opened up your world to your own angels of love and how that experience has changed your life for the better.

Please send your stories to:
<u>info@amanda-hart.co.uk</u>

With love and light always
Amanda

About the Author

Amanda Hart has been an intuitive consultant for over twenty-two years helping people to overcome adversity, to help them find their power and voice.

By helping them to remove the negative programmes that have caused their destructive cycles in various ways, it not only helps them to align to their authentic self, but it awakens them to their innate power, healing and creative expression. Once realigned, clients find their place in this world, their people, their purpose and their peace.

Her memoir *The Guys Upstairs* quite unexpectedly changed her life having battled personally with a turbulent childhood, years of domestic violence, addictions, depression and debilitating conditions post-meningitis. Endorsed by key experts such as Professor Evan Stark (author of *Coercive Control*) and DCI Steve Jackson (National Domestic Abuse Co-Ordinator, College of Policing), she had no idea of the impact that book would have on her personally, as well as others.

Some may know her as one of the finalists on *Britain's Psychic Challenge* on Channel 5, a presenter on My Spirit Radio and columnist for *Soul & Spirit Magazine*. Today she speaks publicly about her story, to help others make sense of theirs.

Amanda works collaboratively with other inspirers from around the world and passionately supports a large global network of women, helping to elevate and empower them to stand out and fully embrace their unique purpose, to make this a better world to live in.

Her message is clear — *'Our purpose unlocks our power and voice. Embracing vulnerability leads us to fear less and love more.'*

Today her books, teaching and her campaign to raise awareness to support those suffering adversities speaks volumes about the kind of determined commitment she has to make this a better world to live in.

Talking with Angels of Light

How to communicate with angels of light and reach your true potential.

Including meditations to connect with your angels of light, space to record the blessings they send you and real accounts of angelic assistance granted to Amanda and her clients over the years. This book will guide you from the shadows of despair and enable you to shine like the purest light in the universe, glowing from the inside out.